Every Step Counts

To Philip, Richard, Paul, Andrew, Mark and Victoria –
our wonderful children. A big thank you to you all for
still loving us and forgiving us so many mistakes
as we tried to parent in our stepfamily.

# Every Step Counts

*Building a healthy stepfamily*

Christine and Tony Tufnell

Text by Christine and Tony Tufnell
Copyright © 2007 Care for the Family

The authors assert the moral right
to be identified as the authors of this work

A Lion Book
an imprint of
**Lion Hudson plc**
Mayfield House, 256 Banbury Road,
Oxford OX2 7DH, England
www.lionhudson.com
ISBN 978 0 7459 5249 9

First edition 2007
10 9 8 7 6 5 4 3 2 1 0

The text paper used in this book has been made from wood
independently certified as having come from sustainable forests

A catalogue record for this book is available
from the British Library

Typeset in 10/14 Latin 725BT
Printed and bound in Great Britain
by Cox & Wyman Ltd, Reading

# Contents

# Stepping together   115

# Introduction

We had been raised in families, we had lived with our children and their other biological parents, and we had experienced single-parent family life, so why would living in a stepfamily be so different? We were soon to learn! Tony has three sons from his previous marriage, and Christine has two sons and a daughter from her previous marriage. So when we married and formed a stepfamily we had six children, five of whom lived with us. They ranged in age from eighteen to four.

Had we understood more about stepfamilies, we would have spared ourselves and our children some of the mistakes we made. It would still have been challenging and tiring, but we would have felt less guilty and more reassured that our stepfamily was normal, that stepfamilies are not the same as nuclear families and that being a step-parent is not the same as being a parent.

We are sharing what we and other stepfamilies have learned, often the hard way, to encourage you in your life in a stepfamily. We are so grateful to all those who shared their stories with us. They are true, but names and identifying details have been changed for anonymity. You may be considering forming a stepfamily, or you may have been living in one for years, but all families change and can grow and develop further. Stepfamilies are formed in many ways but at least one of the couple is a parent. One or both of them may have suffered bereavement, separation or divorce. One may never have lived in a relationship before or may never have parented a child before forming a stepfamily. There may be children living in the stepfamily home all, part, or none of the time. There is no average age for forming a stepfamily – the children may range from 0 to 99! However your family was formed, we hope that you will find much that resonates with you, informs you and gives you ways in which you might move forward in your stepfamily.

Sadly we read most often of those families where things have gone wrong, and there has even been significant harm. Every stepfamily faces difficult situations and not all survive, but we know from those who have shared their stories with us that many have weathered the storms. We want to encourage you that stepfamilies can form healthy relationships and can last. Ours has been going for over twenty years and we are still all speaking to each other!

It is good to remember, especially on bad days, that there are rewards and benefits in being members of a stepfamily!

- We gained a larger family – neither Tony nor Christine have siblings.
- Tony gained a daughter. Girls are definitely different from boys!
- Christine experienced having teenage boys in the house, and learned many lessons before her children reached that age.
- We have enjoyed having a busy family home.
- We shared in wide-ranging conversations round the meal table.
- We know a lot about family weddings.
- Now we include daughters-in-law too; there's plenty of family to visit and who visit us.
- Today we have grandchildren related to Tony, grandchildren related to Christine and grandchildren not related to either of us, all of whom we love.
- Our children tell us that stepfamily life has given them experiences of more parenting styles, more siblings and a model of a lasting couple relationship.

Your benefits and rewards will be different from ours and may be sometime in the future. We cannot make stepfamilies work on our own. All members need to be involved. But if we do our part in building healthy stepfamilies then our lives can be greatly enriched. All our steps matter. Every step counts.

# Foundation steps

# CHAPTER 1

# Complex steps

Stepfamilies are many and varied. The common factor is that one or both of the couple has children from one or several previous relationship(s). These children may live with the couple all, part or none of the time. The partners' experiences may include no previous relationships, short-term relationships, cohabiting relationships, rape, marriage, widowhood, separation or divorce. There may be a mix of any of these.

## Bonding – children and parents

What is common to stepfamilies is that the bonding order, the strength of relationship a member has with another, starts with the children.

In a nuclear family, boy meets girl, they fall in love, cohabit or marry, and then have a child. In this type of family structure, the couple have a history together, an emotional bond or tie, and possibly a legal bond too. When a child is born the parent has a blood bond with the child, a legal bond, and hopefully an emotional one of unconditional love. They begin to share and develop a relationship.

In a stepfamily, the first and strongest bond is between the biological parent and their child. It has history, and is a legal, blood and emotional bond. This parent then meets a new partner. This chosen bond is emotional (passionate love), is growing and deepening, and may become legal too. The weakest bond in a stepfamily is between the step-parent and the stepchild. There is no legal bond, no blood bond and no shared history. The emotional bond will take time and effort from both the step-parent and the stepchild to develop.

> 'Just look at the children's bedrooms. They're such a mess, clothes on the floor, CDs lying around and empty glasses collecting mould. Why can't they hang their clothes in the wardrobe, or put them in the washing basket?' Richard moans about his stepchildren again.
>
> 'Don't get on at them all the time. They'll do their rooms on Saturday. They don't have time during the week,' retorts their mum, Annette. This starts another argument about how Annette always puts the children first and Richard doesn't understand them.
>
> Richard continues, 'Why do we have to fit our arrangements at the weekend round them? It's my weekend too. How about putting me first for a change?'
>
> Annette bursts into tears. 'But I do love you.'

Both Richard and Annette are failing to recognize the different bonding orders in their new family. When a partner already has children, then that partner will tend to take their side in any disagreement. This is even more noticeable if the partner has been living with the children in a single-parent home. Richard has to accept that Annette has children and they are a priority in her life while they are young. This doesn't mean she loves him less, or that he doesn't matter a great deal, rather that in everyday living, the children's needs will often come first. She will tend to organize their activities, and fit her own round them. It will be important for

Annette to stand back and not to take sides with her children against Richard. It would be better for all of them if Richard and Annette discussed ways of parenting together.

> Mary is stepmum to Paul's two daughters. The girls live with their mum, and stay with Paul and Mary alternate weekends. 'Every other weekend, Paul becomes the girls' dad. He drives over a hundred miles to collect them. Laura always needs something new, so they stop off at the 'factory outlet' and Paul spends a small fortune on them both. He says they have to be treated the same. Then they have to eat out. I'm left at home, with the beds to make, the shopping to get and a dinner to cook. Sunday morning they lounge around while I cook dinner again, and then Paul drives them back home. So much for a family weekend. I don't even feel I have a husband.'

Of course Paul wants to spend quality time with his daughters when they stay. He wants to be a good dad. When he was single he could devote all his weekend to his girls. Now he has a wife, but he doesn't want the girls to lose out because he has Mary. Paul's desire to be a good dad and to spend time with his children is great. His bonding with them is strong. But could he and Mary discuss these weekends so that some time is set aside for the girls to have their dad to themselves and some time built in for family fun time to include Mary? Perhaps Mary could sometimes go with Paul to collect the girls and join in the shopping trip, or perhaps they could all go to the cinema, or ten-pin bowling. This would enable the girls and Mary to get to know each other better, and for their bond to grow.

> 'Jack's a lovely boy. He's a charmer like his dad, and even when he's done something wrong it's hard to get cross with him. He's accepted me as part of the family, and confides in me. I was really worried for him last week

when he was rushed into A & E. Thank goodness he wasn't badly hurt in the accident. But I don't love him like I do my own child,' confessed Debbie. 'He's a good kid, and I care about him but it's not the same. Am I an awful stepmum?'

## '… and the greatest of these is love'

Many step-parents echo Debbie's concerns. The English language is very poor when it comes to the word love. In Greek for example there are four words which convey different aspects of love – *philia*, *eros*, *storge* and *agape*.

Debbie has unconditional love for her children. She loved them from the moment they were born and would give her life for them. This is a very strong bond. Debbie loves her new partner too. That love includes friendship and is passionate, intimate and sexual. She hopes it will be lasting. Love for her stepchildren is more tentative. She has to get to know them, and that love will be more like that of love for a close friend – caring, giving and warm. It doesn't have to mean that love is less, but rather that it has different qualities.

## Many relationships

One of the ways of describing family is that it involves relationships, many of which we did not choose! Even a simple family tree will reveal a variety of relatives. In a stepfamily, the number of relationships within the family increases dramatically. It isn't just the couple who relate, or even the step-parent and child, but stepsiblings, step-grandparents and so on.

To work this out mathematically, the number of members in the stepfamily are counted. That number is multiplied by the same number minus one. The result is the number of relationships in the family.

So for a couple with six children between them:

8 x (8 - 1) = 56 relationships

If this couple each have two parents alive and one sibling, the new number of relationships is:

14 x (14 - 1) = 182 relationships!

## Firm and fragile

The children in the stepfamily may also be relating to their other biological parent and their partner and children.

> Sometimes Keith isn't sure how to relate. Who does he obey? Does he have to like all his siblings? Keith lives with his two sisters, his dad, his dad's partner and her child. He visits his mother most weeks. She too has a partner and they have a child. Keith is relating to four adults in parenting positions, two siblings, a stepsibling and a half-sibling.

> When asked about his family, Terry doesn't know what to say. He's the eldest of three children. He lives with his mum and stepdad, and sees his dad during school holidays. His dad moved in with Margaret and her son when he left Terry and Terry's mum. Dad then left Margaret and her son and moved in with Jenny who has two daughters. Now Dad is living with Helen and her daughter. Terry's stepfamily relationships keep changing.

Some of these relationships will have been built since birth, but others are newer and more fragile. By considering the number of relationships in the stepfamily, and especially the number of steps, it is easier to appreciate why forming step-relationships takes time, care and compassion.

For any family to succeed, it needs stability and adaptability. Stability in a stepfamily will take time to achieve, especially given the experiences of at least some of its members that families don't always stay together. Adaptability is a key requisite for everyone in a stepfamily. This family is unique, and will have to adapt, and keep adapting to the changing needs of its members.

**To Think About**

- What are the strongest bonds in your stepfamily?
- How does this affect you and your partner?
- Do you need to accept, discuss or change anything?
- Count the number of members in your stepfamily:
  Multiply that number by the same number, minus 1.
  That number is the number of different relationships in your family.
  How many of these are step-relationships?

# CHAPTER 2

# Steps back

It would be lovely to wipe the slate clean of the past and start afresh with a new relationship. Unfortunately this isn't possible. Everyone carries their past experiences with them. Of course not everything is negative. If Mum and Dad were good enough parents who loved and cared for their child, then this child will grow up with their basic needs met – security, self-worth and identity. If school was a positive experience, and enabled the child to develop and succeed, they will carry this confidence into adult life. Other relationships will also leave their marks for good or ill.

The family that will give the first experience and primary model of family life is the one each person is born into or grows up in. This may be a family with both parents living in it, or a family with only one parent at home, or with foster or adoptive parents. Then there might be older or younger siblings. This experience may then be added to by living alone, living with a partner, living in a two-parent home, living in a single-parent family or living alone again. However, for many people living in a stepfamily today, this will be another new family experience.

'I can see myself now sitting at our dining room table. It was against the wall. Mum sat on one side, Dad sat opposite her, and I sat in the middle. We always had meals sitting at the table. Frequently Mum and Dad weren't speaking to each other, so they spoke only to me. They were very silent meals!' recounted

Joan. 'When I met Vince he was so different – always had plenty to say. After a couple of years he only shouted abuse at me, hit me and threatened to kill me. Now I'm living with Surinda and his son Ajay. I'm so afraid of upsetting anyone. I don't know what to do when Ajay shouts and locks himself in his room.'

Tim remembers his father giving him a jigsaw when he was five years old. 'It was of a farm scene, with a red tractor and a black and white sheep dog. I have this picture of a grey-haired man who made me laugh. I know that my father sent money to my mother, and from time to time he sent me books. He never lived with us. I don't remember meeting him again until I contacted him when I was in my twenties. We met up once. Mum never married again. I've married Jane who has two lovely children, but I don't really know how to be a husband or a father, and I know even less about being a stepdad.'

Susan is one of five children. Her childhood home had been full of laughter and noise. Everyone shouted from time to time to get themselves heard, but after a few sharp exchanges they soon became friends again. 'It was a bit chaotic but there was always someone around to play with. When I got married and had children I thought it would last for ever. It was such a shock when we discovered that my husband had inoperable cancer. He died just a few months later. I never thought I'd meet someone else, but now the children and I live with Peter. He and his daughter like to have everything planned in detail and they are so tidy and quiet. I thought my new family would be like my old one, but it isn't. We're walking round each other as though on egg shells. Peter gets so dejected if I dare to raise my voice. What am I doing wrong?'

Patterns from the past don't have to be repeated, but it takes understanding, awareness of possibilities and conscious effort to create new ones. Recognizing that family experiences have been different is a start. If Joan and Surinda and Susan and Peter share with each other about their past families they will know more about each other and why they react as they do. Then they can decide together what sort of family they would like now. Tim would do well to find out more about marriage and parenting and, perhaps with Jane, attend one of the marriage or parenting courses available.

In forming a stepfamily, at least one of the couple will have had some kind of sexual relationship with someone else. This may have been very short, or lasted for many years.

What happened in this relationship, how it ended and how far the person has worked through the emotions and attachment that they had will affect this stepfamily. There are some aspects which may only surface when they become part of a couple again.

## Building trust

In the UK, the vast majority of stepfamilies are formed after a relationship breakdown. Often trust has been broken by betrayal and abuse. Although the current partner may be innocent of the previous ill-treatment, it will help their partner if they co-operate in being open and in various ways proving that they are trustworthy.

Tom was devastated when his wife went off with his best friend. Now he lives with Sheila. Her work brings her into contact with a number of male colleagues. Whenever possible, she includes Tom in work social events. He knows he can always contact her on her mobile phone. 'We have agreed that if either of us is worried about the other's contact with someone, we will discuss this openly and try to find safeguards that we are both comfortable with.

There's one guy we are both uneasy about when he's with Sheila, so she sees that she's never alone with him. This has really helped me to trust again.'

Mobile phone bills were the thing for Barbara. She had found out about her previous partner's affairs when she saw his mobile phone bill and had rung some of the numbers she didn't recognize. 'It seemed everyone else knew about the affairs except me. I told myself I would never trust another man again. When I met Steve, I was very cautious,' recalls Barbara. Steve said, 'Why did she have to see all my phone bills? I hadn't done anything wrong so at first I resented her checking up on me. Now I just pass the bills over and Barbara is happy.'

## Death of a former partner

For those who have been widowed, there may have been some consolation in keeping things as they were. Queen Victoria had nothing changed in her beloved Albert's rooms for the rest of her life. In fact his study was only moved in 1952. Keeping a shrine like this in a new relationship is not healthy. Putting the important mementos in a memory box would be more appropriate, allowing the past to be recognized but not allowing it to dictate the present.

Fiona became stepmum to Bill's two small children after his wife died. 'I moved into the house that Bill had built for his first wife. Although Bill had got rid of his wife's clothes and other personal things, I'm not allowed to alter anything in what is now our home. He likes everything done the way it has always been. I feel I'm living in someone else's shoes. I feel as though I am never as good as his first wife. The children have accepted me but my marriage isn't what I had hoped it would be.'

**Serin also became a stepmum when Jack's wife died. 'We have worked hard to build a relationship which is special to us. We were able to buy and furnish a new home for us all. It's a bit strained with Jack's first in-laws, but we try to keep in contact as they have lost their daughter and are the children's grandparents. The children do have photos in their rooms of their mum with Jack. This is right for them, but I still don't like looking at them.'**

## Poison from the past

One or both partners may hang on to pain, anger, resentment and bitterness from a past relationship for years. This will infect the current partnership and eventually kill it. Each person needs to find a release from the emotional ties to someone else. Forgiveness of, and release from, this partner will free them to make good connections in this relationship.

## Forgiveness

Forgiveness doesn't always sound right if one has been hurt and abused. Releasing someone could suggest that what they did doesn't matter, and that they can get away with it scot-free. Looking at this the other way round is more relevant here. If someone is unable to forgive they remain tied emotionally to the person who hurt them. There may be a desire to hurt the betrayer but not forgiving them doesn't hurt them. It only damages the one who uses so much emotional energy to keep the anger and other negative feelings alive.

Forgiveness is often a journey and the Reverend David Matthews has expressed it in four steps:

Step one: You say it – 'I will forgive...' Speaking it out loud makes it legal, even if you are struggling to even wish it.

Step two: You mean it. This is engaging your will – you want to forgive.

Step three: You feel it. This may take time, but there is an emotional change and you really mean it.

Step four: You forget it. You won't forget the wrong but you will no longer keep going over it in your mind. The Hebrew word for 'forget' can also mean to 'wither'. Gradually you are no longer struggling to forget; in fact you forget to remember!

# Sexual matters

Finding the time, energy and privacy in a stepfamily for the couple to enjoy a sexual relationship is a challenge. One partner's practice and sexual activity may be very different to those the other partner has had. These past experiences can add to that challenge too: verbal abuse, sexual abuse, different 'norms' and for the 'virgin' various concerns about the partner's experiences and thoughts now.

'Our sexual intimacy was like the rest of our marriage – OK but not exciting,' Barbara explained. 'It was rather dull but we did manage to have three children! He just didn't seem the type to have affairs so I was devastated when I discovered his secret life and he left. Then he tried to divorce me! I was stunned and even more shocked when I read that in his divorce petition he accused me of being frigid.' Barbara has since met Steve. 'I was afraid he would be disappointed in me sexually. I was afraid that there was something wrong with me. Steve has proved that's not true. We have a great sex life!'

Jack feels that he was sexually satisfied in his first marriage. 'We'd been together for some time so I knew her and what would turn her on. She was happy to experiment too. Now with Serin, I'm having to start again.'

And how does Serin see things? 'I'm so aware of Jack's greater sexual experience. I don't feel I can match his expectations. And I'm so tired working and looking after the children. I'm afraid they will barge in or hear us. Having teenagers in the next room is a definite turn-off!'

'I'm finding it hard not to keep imagining Jane with other people. She's my first love so it's all very precious to me. I feel that she's tainted in some way and that I'm second best,' Tim said. 'Jane says I'm different. I talk quietly to her, and want to learn what arouses her. I guess that when we've been together longer I will get more confidence. It's easier when the children stay with her mum and dad.'

Carol is struggling in a different way. 'My son was born as a result of date rape. My drink had been spiked. I have mixed feelings about being touched again. Although Sean is a very gentle man, and a great stepdad, I'm not always very kind to him. I'll go so far and then I'll shout, "No" and push him away. I'm having counselling to help me with this.'

It isn't always easy to talk about such private matters, but sharing together is the way forward. Professional counselling might be needed too.

## Repeating the past

There is a danger that those with ex-partners may repeat the patterns of the past, choosing someone with similar characteristics, or not accepting responsibility for their part in past failures. For example: women who repeatedly marry abusers, or men who blame their ex-wives for all their faults. This is outside the remit of this book, but agencies listed in the resources at the end may be helpful.

## Children's experiences

The children bring their past experiences of family life with them too. They may have lived with both birth parents, lived in a single-parent family all or some of the time, lived part of the time with Mum and part of the time with Dad, and lived in a previous stepfamily, or live in another stepfamily now. All these experiences will colour the way they view this step-parent and this stepfamily.

Uncertainty and wariness are common reactions. Given that biological Mum and biological Dad's relationship didn't last, they have no way of knowing that this relationship will last either. Other experiences may compound this view. To have one's mother leave, even if there were valid reasons, does shake the core being of a child.

According to the Archbishop of Canterbury, Rowan Williams, biological fathers have a choice whether to actively parent or not. They are not compelled physically to be involved in the same way as the birth mother! This choice means that for a child whose father does not have a parenting relationship with them, they will feel 'not chosen' and thus rejected.

The death of a parent may not have been anyone's fault, but to the child this confirms the uncertainty of life. If one parent died, will the other one live? Will the step-parent die too?

There may have been many positive experiences of family in the child's life which will equip them to make the adjustments necessary to be part of a stepfamily. However, many children will have suffered negative aspects of family which they may carry into this stepfamily. They too may have been verbally, physically or sexually abused or witnessed their parent suffering this.

> 'It was a family outing that made me realize how careful I needed to be.' Tim went on to describe the occasion. 'We were travelling in the car. I was driving, Jane was next to me, and the children were in the back. We arrived at a town we had never been to before. There was a lot of traffic and a one-way system to negotiate. I asked Jane to look for signs to a car park. She called for me to turn left, but it was far too late for me to change lanes. We had a little barney! We did find a car park and Jane and I forgot about the heated words we had exchanged. We were keen to see the place. However, Molly, who is six, was unusually quiet. "Is something wrong?" I asked. "Are you going to hit Mummy like Daddy did?" was her question.'

> Rosie and her mum had been on their own since Rosie was born. Now Bob has moved in. 'It's odd to see shaving things in the bathroom. And why does he always leave the toilet seat up?' Rosie was full of questions. 'Why can't I get into your bed when I wake up in the middle of the night? Why do you lock your bedroom door? Why can't I run around without getting dressed first? Why do we always have to ask Bob before we do anything? Why do we have to have shepherd's pie for dinner, which I hate, just because he likes it? Why do we have to have a man living with us?'

The children may have very mixed feelings about living in a stepfamily. They may still be angry about the break-up of their original family. Anger is often an emotion that follows being hurt or not getting one's own way. The child may resent having to live in a stepfamily as it's not what they would choose. It is possible that the child is blaming themself for their parent leaving or dying. They may even feel they didn't try hard enough to get their parents back together again. So they may bring with them into this family anger, guilt and confusion.

Although all these past experiences will affect everyone, it is the quality of relationships that will finally determine the outcome of the stepfamily.

**To Think About**

- What are your experiences of family life?
- In the light of these, what changes would you like to make in the way you interact with your partner and your stepchildren?
- Are there things from your past which are hindering your current relationship?
- What experience of family has each child brought into your stepfamily?

# CHAPTER 3

# Realistic steps

Building a stepfamily is not the same as building a nuclear family. Just as the fairy stories of *Cinderella* and *Hansel and Gretel* aren't true, neither are TV stepfamilies like *The Brady Bunch*, nor novels and videos like *Stepmom*. Dreams of the perfect stepfamily and of being the perfect stepmum or stepdad are just dreams. Expecting too much of ourselves or of others leads to failure and guilt when those standards haven't been reached. It's then possible to think that the stepfamily isn't working out because it isn't what was expected. Those thoughts can lead to a sense of hopelessness, which in turn can lead to the break-up of the stepfamily. Being realistic about living in a stepfamily gives a framework in which to grow and develop without trying to reach for unobtainable goals. It also helps to reduce the guilt which seems to go with being a parent or step-parent.

It is a false expectation that stepfamily members will love each other because the couple love each other and that there will be complete harmony. No family gets on together all the time. Love takes time to grow. There may not always be love between the members of a stepfamily, but there can be care and respect for each other.

## Respect

Respect for each other is very important in a stepfamily. If the adults and the children can respect each other, even when they don't like each other very much, or don't love each other, then the family can function. The danger is that without respect, the relationships will deteriorate, and any conversations become a series of 'put downs'.

## Challenges and uncertainties

All stepfamilies have challenges to face. Some things are easier in one family than another but that doesn't make one type of stepfamily less stressful than another.

It will be different for the family where the former partner died. There is no ongoing contact but there is the possibility that the deceased has become a 'saint' in the minds of their partner and the children. One person's second husband said, 'There's no one so perfect as your wife's dead first husband.'

It may seem easier if the children don't live with the couple for much of the time. It's true that there is more time for the couple to be alone to develop their relationship. However, the changes that happen when the children visit or stay are great. The biological parent may devote themself to the children when they visit because they are not there all the time. The step-parent may feel left out, or required to do lots of extra work like cooking and washing. It takes longer for step-parent and stepchild to build a relationship. Sometimes the child comes to live permanently with this couple and they face that change too.

Some joys and struggles are common to all families, however they are formed. Toddler tantrums and moody teenagers are known to all parents! All parents get exasperated at times, and are relieved when their offspring are in bed. All children think that their parents are 'wrinklies', and don't understand their generation. Discussions over pocket money, choice of clothes, doing homework and late nights out are a part of parenting. So are worries about the children's health, choice of friends, drugs, teenage pregnancy and 'going off the rails'.

## Parenting priorities

Experience of raising children and their stages of development will certainly help. Being a parent already does mean having some understanding of the demands of bringing up a child. But a stepchild has a history that the step-parent isn't part of. The child has already been parented by one or both biological parents, and possibly by grandparents or other step-parents too. This parenting may be very different from the way the step-parent is parenting their own child. The role of a step-parent is not the same as that of the biological parent. It will be dependent on a number of factors like age, experience and personality.

> 'My stepdaughter and stepson were nine and seven and lived with their mum and stepdad. Both families were in the military so we were constantly moving around and it was impossible for any regular contact between the children and their dad. In the early days I was jealous and resentful of the way they seemed to dominate my husband's time when they were with us. I seemed to have no aptitude for the practical side of parenting. When we were on our own together, the children and I downed copious amounts of coke, ice-cream and sweets for our tea. We all loved it, but in retrospect it was not the healthiest diet!'

It isn't possible to be perfect! Many want to be the best parent or step-parent they can be and that's fine. It's important to recognize one's limitations too. Being a 'good enough' parent or step-parent is a realistic aim.

Marriage does change things, but it is not the answer to all the problems. Some things get better and others seem to get worse! One of the reasons people get married is to make a public declaration of their commitment to each other. This can give the children a greater sense of security and of being a part of a family unit. However, it also signals the end of any hope the child might have had that biological Mum and Dad might get back together again. If a child hates the prospective step-parent, marriage won't change this. If the step-parent didn't like the children before they married the children's parent, they won't like living with them now. The children may be worried that this couple relationship means that they will be less loved.

Some step-parents decide that it would be better and easier if their partner is totally responsible for bringing up the children. This opt-out step-parent is heading for resentment from their partner, and a disunited family. One person may do more – perhaps the one who stays at home to care for the children while the other one goes out to work. But if involvement in the children's lives is not shared then this could quickly become a major frustration for either person or both of them. Either 'I'm doing it all and you don't help' or 'I'm just the lodger in this family.'

To expect that the stepfamily will not be affected in any way by the children's other parent is totally false. Every stepfamily is affected by the other parent of the child member. Even if the child has no contact with their other birth parent, and may even not know who that is, they will carry some of the effects of this in their lives. This is similar to those children who have been adopted, about whom there has been much more research. Acceptance of this influence is necessary. It may be unfair, especially to the new partner, but the children do have another parent. To the stepfamily, this impact may be negative or positive, or a mixture of both. The stepfamily has to find ways to preserve its identity and make any contact as non-confrontational as it can.

## Conflict and the longer term

It is realistic to look for rewards in building a stepfamily. However, these usually come after much time and effort. There may be some rewards now – a good couple relationship, having a family when they didn't think they would, having a larger family, enjoying the children. Longer term rewards may include close relationships with steps, seeing children mature and having grandchildren. Healthy relationships can be built, but they need the co-operation of both parties.

To assume that a stepfamily will form a healthy unit quickly is false. It is estimated that it takes between four and six years for a stepfamily to form a cohesive unit which functions satisfactorily. Jan Lawton, a research psychologist at the University of Queensland, found that 'The divorce rate among remarried families is high in the first two years – then it slows down. By about the five-year period, second relationships are more stable then first relationships. I see these couples as very high risk during the first few years, but thereafter offering great benefits to the children.' There is good news if everyone is prepared to work at building relationships and accepts that these will take time to achieve.

## Settling down

One way of describing a stepfamily is to use an adapted model of group development devised by Bruce C. Tuckman: 'Forming, Storming, Norming and Performing'. Of course, not all stepfamilies fit this neat pattern but it does give an idea of the stages that most stepfamilies go through to become healthy stepfamilies.

### Stage 1: Forming

The forming stage of a stepfamily is when everyone is on their best behaviour. So when the prospective new partner meets the children everyone tries really hard to get along. Children are sometimes told to be on their best behaviour when they meet... Most adults too want to create a good impression. This might be for the first few meetings, but can last until the family has lived together for a little while. All seems to be going well initially, and when conflict arises it surprises everyone.

### Stage 2: Storming

This stage may last for some time in a stepfamily. Here conflicts and frustrations within the family come up. They may be suppressed for a while and form an undercurrent. The step-parent may keep quiet so they don't 'rock the boat', but they are discovering how much harder it is to live with children than they expected. The children may be being children – noisy, messy, argumentative, naughty. And the couple are also still finding out about each other and the areas where they clash. It is important to acknowledge the disagreements and find ways to resolve them as far as possible. Given all the possible relationships in stepfamilies, it may take a while to find solutions and a workable way forward.

### Stage 3: Norming

Family members have got to know each other better. The 'shape' of this family has been established, with rules and boundaries.

Shared memories and traditions grow. This family may still resent and resist outside influences as it is not yet strong enough to feel secure. It may be hesitant to acknowledge to the world that it is a stepfamily. It is a working unit but not yet secure. There are challenges but the family is better equipped to face them.

### Stage 4: Performing

Here the stepfamily is a cohesive, identifiable unit, with each member having a sense of belonging, of being cared about, of having a place in it and a loyalty to it. This is the goal of a successful stepfamily.

'I didn't know what I was letting myself in for when I married her. I thought she would go on looking after the kids as she had done before. She was OK but it was the kids. She put the children first and everything revolved round them. There was no room for me.' Ian went on, 'We started arguing all the time. Then her ex didn't always pay on time. Kids cost a fortune. I never liked her son anyway. We split up after eighteen months.'

Looking back, Mary says, 'If I had known some of this when I remarried, I would have saved myself a lot of grief. I tried to make my stepfamily like my nuclear one. It was such hard work. I thought I was failing as a stepmum. I resented any contact with the children's mother. With more understanding I am easier on myself and much easier on my stepchildren. Now I'm not trying to achieve the impossible. I believe we will make it.'

Realistic expectations are important at all stages of stepfamily life. They can give hope and aims without condemning the family to failure.

**To Think About**

* What 'stage' has your stepfamily reached?
* Do you want to change any of your expectations about your stepfamily?
* How might you see and do things differently in your stepfamily?

# Tandem steps

# CHAPTER 4

# The step-couple

The quality of the couple relationship is paramount to the success of the stepfamily. If this is a committed, loving relationship it will withstand all the pressures that it will face living in a stepfamily. If this relationship is insecure and weak, then it is more likely to buckle under the strain of stepfamily life.

Dr Francesca Adler-Baeder, author of *Smart Steps* (a research-based Family Life Education Program Curriculum for couples and children forming stepfamilies, published by the Stepfamily Association of America), says that, 'All issues in a stepfamily – even those in the other biological parent's household – ripple back to the step-couple.'

This is why in a book on stepfamilies, a whole section is devoted to the couple. They are building their relationship in front of the children all or part of the time. With so many demands on their time and energy made by the children, their partnership can be overlooked. Sadly the children are often given as the reason for a relationship breakdown. If disagreements over parenting styles are not resolved, then intimacy between the couple suffers.

'Building a stepfamily is like working on a car engine while it is still running,' is how Gordon Taylor, co-author of *Designing Dynamic Stepfamilies*, described it at the Smart Marriages Conference in Dallas, Texas, 2005. This suggests hard work, danger and the possibility that it will run away from you. There are lots of parts to work on at the same time, and they all matter. But in a stepfamily, working on parenting without giving time and attention to the couple is like cleaning the spark plugs without putting oil in the engine. It won't work.

The traditional wedding vows say 'until death do us part'. This vow may have already been broken for one partner. Love has not lasted for forever. Death may have come early, and so that love has changed. Love and commitment are the foundations for good relationships.

Gary Chapman in his book, *The Five Love Languages*, writes, 'Though the "falling-in-love" experience is exciting, it is short-lived and largely self-centred. Love that truly contributes to our spouse's emotional well-being is based on reason, will, and discipline.' That is a challenging description at any time, but living in a stepfamily will mean determination too, to give priority to this loving relationship above self, giving it time and energy.

There are times when it's very easy to think of all the things that one loves about one's partner. Making a list of all the partner's lovable qualities and keeping it handy is a good reminder. Reading it again on those days when love seems far away can help.

## Sharing life beliefs

Research into the couple relationship in a stepfamily has found that marriage is still marriage! It hasn't changed – it still needs all the attention, skill and understanding of any first-time marriage. But it does have added pressures. Preparation for marriage with children from a previous relationship would help.

A study, as yet unpublished, by Ron Deal, director of Successful Stepfamilies, and David Olsen, director of Prepare/Enrich, has revealed some interesting predictors for the success of further marriages. Sharing life beliefs, like why we are here, and what the point of life is, has been shown to be a big key in predicting the happiness and satisfaction in a further marriage. Also rated as very important is communication, and sharing leisure activities. Personality, family and friends are part of this too.

## Communicating

Communication is vital in all relationships. If the couple can find ways of communicating between themselves which are constructive and effective, then this will not only be good for their relationship but will also equip them to handle parenting and step-parenting issues.

When two people first meet and start to get to know each other, there always seems so much to talk about. One shares and the other is keen to learn all they can about their new love. Time and living together dulls this enthusiasm. Just like the stages of development of the stepfamily, relationships go through stages too. The pattern that most frequently emerges is that she will complain that he no longer listens as she works out her feelings by talking, while he feels he has heard it all before, nods and either looks for an immediate solution or retreats to consider what to do next. It's all too easy to get into a cycle of attack and counter-attack. Both get hurt and nothing gets resolved.

## Ways to communicate

The stalemate needs to be broken. Here are two well-known and very effective ways to re-open and keep open those communication channels.

## 1. Taking turns to talk

Set aside time to talk and find a suitable place. Make sure this is a time when neither is too tired and there won't be any interruptions. Initially, choose one issue to discuss that doesn't immediately make emotional temperatures rise dramatically. Consider topics that need a resolution, like why one person is always late, and the other hates having to wait, or what type of family holiday can be agreed upon, when one wants to go camping as a family and the other wants to go to a hotel and leave the children elsewhere.

A cushion or similar soft object is required. The rule is that only the person holding the cushion may speak. The other person listens so that they can repeat back what they have heard, to check that what they think they heard is what the other person thinks they said. The issue under discussion can be written on a piece of paper and put on the floor or table between the couple. This is as a reminder that the problem is out there, and not part of one person. Starting sentences with 'I feel', rather than 'You make me...' will also help each one to be less defensive and less angry.

So one person holds the cushion and talks first. When they have finished, they pass the cushion to the other person. This one checks with the first speaker that they have understood what the speaker was saying. If the first speaker does not feel understood, then the cushion passes back and they explain further.

Only when the first speaker is assured that the other person has understood them, can that partner talk and share their views. This talker now checks that they have been understood.

This process continues so that both partners' views are understood. It is then easier to empathize and find ways to resolve the issue.

Whenever they were going out as a family, Richard would get cross. 'Why can't you get ready on time? You're always late. Now we'll be late for the cinema.' Then he would go and sit in the car with the engine running. The children would hear the raised voice and get in the car quietly. Annette would rush around and mutter to herself. The journey would start in silence.

'We tried out the "cushion" idea using a balloon!' says Annette. 'When we stopped to listen and explain it became clearer. Richard was used to only getting himself ready for an outing. He liked to be early for everything, because he was in trouble as a boy if he was late. As for me, I would get the children ready first and then get myself ready in whatever time was left. I also saw that the dog had water in her bowl, had been out into the garden, and that the back door was now locked. The more Richard revved the engine, the more flustered I got.

'We are trying out a new pattern. I get the children and myself ready, and Richard sees to the dog and locking up.'

## 2. Writing it down

Writing a letter gives time for the writer to think about how they are going to express their thoughts and feelings, and for strong emotions to slow down a bit. It allows for changes to be made so that the meaning is clearer. The writer can put everything down without being interrupted by their partner. They may even tear up some attempts as being too angry and unkind. It can be especially helpful when the issue is a very emotive one, or when it isn't possible for a while to speak privately to the partner. The receiver of the letter can consider all the points before replying either verbally or in another letter.

The rules are that the letter must start with praise of the partner. The list of lovable traits might help here. Sentences must start with

'I feel... when...' and should not contain 'you make me...' or 'you always...'.

> Debbie says, 'David works long hours, so finding time together when his son and my daughter were not around was difficult. We would start talking late at night about us and the children. I would get upset and David would get angry. Then he would want to go to sleep as he had to be up early in the morning. I was left all tense and frustrated. I discovered that by writing a letter to David for him to read next morning, I could finish expressing how I felt. Then it was easier for me to sleep too! It also gives David the opportunity to think about things without getting so worked up. It has really helped us in our relationship and with parenting.'

## Having fun!

Everyone needs hobbies – leisure activities that allow rest, relaxation, a change from work and most of all, fun. With a busy family life, time and money for individual and couple activities are in short supply. Some things may have to wait till the children are older, or retirement. Others can be adapted to fit in the schedule. Fun and laughter produce endorphins which give a feeling of well-being. So things which are enjoyable should be included in the couple and the family diary.

## Making time to be together

Opportunity to be together to talk, to be close and to give each other attention is vital. This means more than sitting watching TV in the same room. It means making time for each other frequently. In a stepfamily, it often means planning ahead and booking a 'date' with each other. Given the range of ages and needs in a stepfamily, finding quality time as a couple is a challenge. If there seems to be no space, create it, even taking a day off work while the children are at school so that the couple can be alone without interruption.

## Individual space

Space for individual 'time out' is needed too. For the good of the couple, each person needs their own space. Some will read a novel, some will garden, others will go for a walk by themselves, or go to the gym or play golf. As long as these pursuits don't exclude the partner and family for too long, they will be beneficial.

Barbara and Steve keep alternate Saturdays for themselves. Barbara's children stay with their father on alternate weekends, so this makes a good time for them to be together. Steve says, 'We get up late, and often have lunch out. We like walking in the country whatever the weather. It's lovely to have a whole day to ourselves.'

Both Mary and Paul work, and Mary works some weekends too. They enjoy being involved in their local scout troop but this takes up a lot of their free time. They have Paul's girls to stay alternate weekends, and for holidays. 'The only night we are always free is Monday so we keep that as our night. I have blocked it off in my diary so if anyone phones asking if I'm available I can easily say no,' explains Mary.

'Our family timetable didn't have any slots just for us,' says Norman. Jill's youngest is only five years old, and Norman's eldest is eighteen, and there are four more children in between. He continues, 'It was a real struggle to find any time. Only some of our children have contact with their other parent. Occasionally Jill's parents will have the younger children to stay for a night. The older ones can be left for a few hours. So when this happens we treat ourselves and enjoy a meal out together.'

Jill adds, 'On a regular basis, we've found Saturday mornings are good for catching up on each other's week, and sorting anything out between us. Everyone laughs that we spend the morning sitting in bed talking – with a cup of tea of course. But the teenagers sleep till midday, and the younger ones are happy watching TV.'

## Intimacy

Time and energy for a satisfying sexual life is vital too. There are a number of good books about improving sexual intimacy. Reading and discussing some of these may give some fresh ideas and new slants. There will be some things that can be unique to this relationship – different foreplay, positions and surroundings. Scented candles, soft, sensual blankets, low lights and music can all add to the atmosphere.

Looking after young children is physically tiring. They can also get in the way of intimate contact. A child will often walk along between the couple holding a hand of each of them. They will climb onto a lap just when the couple are sitting close together. At night, they have nightmares, or are sick just as the couple are enjoying foreplay. They want to get into bed with the couple early in the morning. A lock on the bedroom door is a solution for many couples. Others persuade grandparents to have the youngsters to stay for a night. Others guard the times when the children are with their other parent as quality time for their relationship.

Teenagers can be inhibiting too. It is often uncomfortable for teenagers to be faced with evidence of their parents' sexual lives.

'Ugh', 'disgusting', 'revolting', 'gross' are some of the words they may use. So any display of intimacy is likely to be looked upon with horror. If they are finding it hard to accept the step-parent, they may be even more antagonistic. Especially for Stepmum, if there's any chance that the couple could be overheard or seen while love-making she is likely to be highly embarrassed. Fortunately teenagers often go out in the evenings, sleep late at weekends and like loud music! When parenting teenagers, it may mean being spontaneous and taking opportunities to be intimate together whenever they arise.

## Time, effort and success

'We just focused on the wedding and all the other stuff was overlooked. We didn't realize how difficult it was going to be, and how dramatic the changes would be. Because we were in love we thought that it would be OK. It's been hard making our relationship work because of baggage from the past. It is taking loyalty and lots of give and take,' says Annette.

Richard adds, 'The children are a challenge too. I had no idea how much time it takes to look after them. There have been times when I've felt like giving up. Then I go and put my arms round Annette and know we'll make it.'

'I find little notes to say how much she loves me in with my sandwiches when I'm at work,' says David. 'They mean so much to me. I know that Debbie has thought of me when she made my lunch the night before. I see putting the rubbish out, cleaning her car and providing for her as ways I show her that I love her. And buying the occasional bunch of flowers! I do tell her as often as I can that I love her.'

Just thinking about the time and effort needed for the couple relationship to grow and strengthen might seem too much. Add to this all the challenges of parenting and step-parenting and being single or a single parent might seem easier! It would certainly be simpler. However, the couple have chosen to be together and there are all the wonderful benefits of being in a loving, committed relationship. To be loved, cared about, protected, secure, trusted, accepted, to be close to and to matter to someone, is priceless. There are stresses in a stepfamily, and recognizing these and finding ways to reduce as many as possible will help. People are often surprised by the additional pressures that come when living in a stepfamily. It is one of the reasons why couple relationships break down. Building and maintaining a committed, strong, loving couple relationship is key to building and maintaining a healthy stepfamily.

**To Think About**

• Use this paraphrase of the wedding vows to renew your commitment to each other:

> *I choose to love you:*
> *Whatever happens*
> *However I feel*
> *Whoever I meet*
> *Whenever we have problems*
> *Whether or not I feel in love.*
> **(Care for the Family: Connect 2)**

• Draw up a weekly timetable for each member of your family. Are there family times, couple times and individual space times? Is a better balance needed?

- What can you do to make this sexual relationship a unique and satisfying one?
- What are the stresses you face together/as parents/as step-parents/as individuals?
- Are there any creative ways in which you could work together to reduce some of the stresses in your stepfamily?

# CHAPTER 5

# Practical steps

Money, home and wills are three areas of stepfamily life to consider. These practical matters do affect how people feel, and can cause either conflict or a sense of belonging.

According to Sheryl Nance-Nash writing in an article called 'Managing a Blended Family' in *Black Enterprise*, 'Poor planning and disagreement on goals can quickly unravel recently constituted stepfamilies. For one thing, the second or third time around, finances can be an even greater issue since both spouses usually have more assets, more debts and contradictory money-management styles… the children may have very different spending habits and values.'

It's not just where the family lives geographically that matters but how they view this home. To start out living as a stepfamily in a new house, with new furniture, and with all family members having input is great. Everyone would be starting out together as equals, settling down together in new surroundings with no previous memories attached to the place. Money, or lack of it, jobs, the children's schooling, and lack of planning mean this doesn't usually happen. One partner, with or without children, moves into the existing home of the other partner. This solution may solve the immediate need to live together, but there are practical issues which need to be worked out and these involve feelings too. Not doing this will leave one partner, and possibly the children too, feeling that at best they are guests, or at worst, unwelcome lodgers in someone else's home. Moving into an existing home can work very well if everyone is prepared to make adjustments, and find ways in which everyone can feel 'this is our home now'.

> 'Although I did move into her home when we first got married, we knew that this was temporary. As soon as we had sold my flat and then sold her flat, we bought a house of our own. I must say it is lovely to have everything as "ours". The children took the move OK as they have stayed at the same school. I thought this would make us a united stepfamily but it hasn't! It has helped but there are still other issues to work through,' Bob says.

## Whose home?

Traditionally, the home was seen as the woman's domain. Whilst this is not a widely accepted view today, women still tend to be home-makers, investing a lot of emotional as well as creative energy in building a comfortable environment for the family to live in.

They tend too to have a more sentimental attachment to places and things. This is a generalisation, as both partners can find living in the other's existing home a constant reminder of a time when they were not part of the family, and a previous partner may have once lived there too. It's not just bricks and mortar, but household items like furniture, china and bedding which may still be in use.

It is for the partner whose home it was originally to make the new partner feel welcome and included. It's not enough to say there's space in the wardrobe, and empty drawers for their things. It means taking a step back and looking at the house or flat with fresh eyes. If this person was moving into this house now with this new partner and the children, how would things be arranged? It's never too late to discuss how people feel about the home, and what changes are possible so that everyone takes ownership of it.

> **When Abigail moved into Koyo's house it was so obviously male! She says, 'There weren't any plants or ornaments or photos around. Almost every room was the same dull colour. Some furniture and things had been taken by Koyo's ex-wife when she left, so we replaced them with some of my things and with second-hand stuff. The local post office notice board was a convenient place to find reasonably good furniture. I didn't like having to stay in the same master bedroom, so I tried not to think about it and concentrated on enjoying being with Koyo. Koyo's boys were able to stay in their original bedrooms.'**

## Where we all sleep

There may not be much room for manoeuvre about where everyone sleeps. The larger size of stepfamilies and the accommodation available often decree who will sleep with whom and where. This may need reviewing from time to time as the children get older, or the couple have a child from this relationship. Redecorating bedrooms, letting the children have a say in the colour scheme or fabrics used, goes a long way to establishing that 'this bedroom is mine/ours'.

The children who are part of this stepfamily but who only stay some of the time need to feel they belong too. Space may be at a premium, but giving them part of a room, a drawer or even a box for the things they keep in this home helps them to feel included. Personal, everyday items should be there too like toothbrushes, flannels, toys and books.

A new bed or bed linen for the master bedroom is another priority – sleeping in sheets that have been used by the previous couple is not conducive to intimacy! However, sharing other things from both former homes may be practical as well as demonstrating the merger. More people in the family means more crockery, cutlery and cookware is needed. Ornaments and pictures which mean a lot to one person can be included.

## Creating the home

Buying second-hand furniture together if money is tight will still involve joint decisions and an opportunity to create this family home. Items one person is not ready to dispose of can be stored in the attic or garage. This gives time for that person to decide at a later date if they still want it or if the time has come to move on and get rid of the object.

'I always felt like a lodger. Perhaps that's why we're not together now,' Ian sadly shares. 'I moved into her house. Her daughters didn't really accept me. Although I had some space for my clothes in the bedroom, there was nothing else in the house that was mine or even belonged to both of us. It was as if everyone wanted to go on as before with me as an extra. I was always the outsider.'

'I needed to move things round in the kitchen,' explains Mary. 'I'm not very tall and so need everyday items within my reach. I moved plates and mugs to lower shelves, and bought a pair of kitchen steps. Paul and the children couldn't find things for a bit but they didn't complain. Perhaps they were enjoying my home cooking! It really helped when Paul told me it was my home and I could do as I liked. He had to tell me frequently before I began to believe him!'

Front door keys signify ownership, and a right of entrance. These can be given to all the members of the stepfamily old enough to be responsible. Gradually this house or flat will become emotionally as well as practically 'our home'.

## Money matters

Money, or the lack of it, is another important area to discuss. Rob Parsons, in his book *The Money Secret* writes, 'over seventy per cent of couples who split up give money problems as their number one reason'. In a stepfamily there may be extra pressures on the family income. How the finances are arranged and who pays for what can be worked out to suit both partners. Sometimes it is the emotional aspects behind how the money is apportioned or spent that are harder to see and find a way through.

Money is neither good nor bad! A biblical saying is often misquoted and should read, 'the *love* of money is a root of all kinds of evil' (1 Timothy 6:10). People tend to fall into two groups – the impulsive, spontaneous group or the careful, budgeting, planning group. If the couple is formed from one of each group, then understanding how the other operates will help in working towards a solution without conflict.

In a stepfamily there may be some ongoing financial commitments to another family, or some income which is derived from an absent parent. This can seem very unfair when a current couple sees either that money is going outside their family, or that they do not receive what is due to them for the children living with them.

Child support or maintenance, either given or received, can be a complex subject. In Britain, a parent is responsible for contributing to the support of their child whether the child lives with them or not and this is dealt with by the Child Support Agency (CSA). Although maintenance can be arranged between the two parents without recourse to the CSA, frequently the amount to be paid has been assessed by them. This could even include a past step-parent who had been supporting the child and is required to continue to do so.

> **Joanne battles with resentment: 'I work very hard and so does Simon. We want to start a family of our own but we can't afford it. Simon pays a lot in maintenance to his ex-wife for the children but she is always finding ways to get more. The boys needed a new computer to do their school work and we were expected to buy it. Of course Simon did. I struggle with all this, but I'm learning to look at it in another way. Simon is such an honourable person that he would do his best for his children. I think he'll make a good dad for our children one day too.'**

Accepting a situation that for whatever reason doesn't seem fair isn't easy, but will be necessary if there isn't to be constant anguish over child support payments. The CSA can reassess the amount if there has been a change in circumstances.

## Be aware of favouritism

It is very important that all the children are treated as similarly as possible, whether they live most of the time in the family or not. Conflict arises between the couple and between the children if some of the children are favoured more than others with clothes, toys and outings. If there is a good reason for differences then these need explaining to the children.

'We just had to explain to Harry and Chloe that we couldn't give them all that Daniel has.' Andy continues, 'It is unfair, but Daniel gets lots of presents from his dad's family and we can't afford to give our two the same. It's hard on them all. We try to find ways of treating Harry and Chloe when Daniel's with his grandparents which make them feel special too but which don't cost too much. They know Daniel's dad died so we hope they understand a bit.'

## Budgeting

Talking about income and expenditure and working out a budget will go a long way in sorting out the emotional baggage of resentment, jealousy and insecurity. This may need to be adjusted over time to account for the changes in the family.

'I'm definitely the spender! I love going shopping and buying new clothes for the children. I don't want them to suffer because I took them away from their dad. My ex is well paid so there was always plenty of money,' explains Annette. 'Although I work part-time, we don't have so much money now and we're buying our house. Richard is much better at budgeting than I am. We have decided that I can spend the Child Support money on the children in any way I see fit. But I don't have any credit cards so I'm not tempted to overspend.'

'When we got married, we decided who should pay for what. Five years later, with the children now teenagers, money is a bit tight so we're trying to spend less,' shares Isaiah. 'As we both think the other one of us could budget better, we're trying a month of role reversal! I'm doing all the food and household supplies shopping and my wife is looking after the household bills. We hope this will help us to understand each other better and agree new budgets.'

# Where there's a will...

Making a will is not usually on the top of a list of things to do but in a stepfamily it is strongly advised. However the family has been formed, consult a solicitor about making a will. This is not to be morbid but to make the best provision for the family, so that those one wants to inherit actually do so.

Marriage automatically revokes any former wills that either partner may have made.

If a married person dies in the UK without making a will, the way in which their assets are dealt with is governed by an Act of Parliament. What happens depends on the value of the estate, and the result can be very different than they might have intended. Their assets will not automatically pass to the surviving husband or wife, but may be distributed between them and others including parents, brothers and sisters. This may mean that blood children, adopted children and stepchildren are dealt with differently too. Stepchildren must be named in a will if they are to inherit. Those cohabiting will need to be clear about home ownership and so forth too.

These practical steps do count. They will help a stepfamily work together or they can pull it apart.

**To Think About**

- What are your views about your family finances?
- What are your partner's?
- Do these differences need addressing?
- As a step-couple have you made new wills, or do you need to discuss this further?

# Family steps – parenting

# CHAPTER 6

# Being Stepmum
# or Stepdad

Parenting and step-parenting are different. Parents have a blood, legal and emotional tie to their children. Step-parents only have an emotional tie, and this may not be very strong. The Old English word for step is 'stēop' which means loss, and so whenever a child has a step-parent there has been a loss or bereavement. So step-parents don't start from a good place!

Fairy stories about wicked stepmothers and a general feeling in society that stepfathers are abusive don't help either. Most step-parents want to do their best and try really hard to parent and care for their stepchild.

Originally, stepmothers did replace the mother who had died, often in childbirth. Dad needed someone to care for his children and so often married again. Until the twentieth century, it was very difficult for women to divorce and children remained the property of their father. Today many stepfamilies are formed following the breakdown of a relationship rather than following the death of a spouse.

## Roles in step-parenting

The role of a step-parent changes with each situation and child. It changes as the child and family matures too! There are times when it is that of a substitute parent, a friend, an auntie or uncle figure, a mentor, a parent's partner, or a significant person in the child's life. In fact there is no one definition which fits all step-parents. The following from Tony Parsons' *Man and Boy* illustrates this:

> 'But I didn't know if I was meant to be her friend or her father, if I was meant to be sweetness and light or firm but fair. None of it felt right. When your partner has got a child, it can never be like the movies. And anyone who can't see that has watched a few too many MGM musicals.'

The age of the stepchild and that child's experiences and relationship with the same sex biological parent will determine much of the step-parent's role. The personality of the step-parent and their willingness or otherwise to be involved in the child's life will also shape that role.

Younger children are more likely to accept another parent figure in their lives. Many will talk of having two dads or two mums. This may not be how the biological parent sees it! However, if the adults can accept this, the child can feel affirmed and loved by all their parents. If the child has little or no contact with one of their biological parents, then the step-parent might step into that parent's place up to a point.

> 'John and I were shopping recently. He's my stepson, now five, and we've been a stepfamily for eighteen months,' explains Phil. 'We went into the supermarket. We were just chatting as I picked up things for lunch. Suddenly John said, "I'm not going to call you Phil anymore. I have a new name for you." I was thinking, "What's he going to call me now?" "I'm going to call you Dad."
>
> It's Vicky, John's mum, who is finding this so hard. 'I've never called

anyone "Dad" to John. John's biological father is just referred to as "your father" so he hasn't had a dad before.'

# Teen children

Teenagers are already moving away from dependency on their parents for all their needs to be met. There is a change in the parent/child relationship through these years. So the step-parent of a teenager is less likely to be a parent/authority figure. If the relationship grows, it may become somewhere between friend and mentor.

Jill's stepsons were in their teens when she married their dad. 'I know that I can't be the boys' mother – they already have a mother. But my role is one of mothering. As they live with us, I cook, wash and shop. I care for them and look after them when they're ill. I'm not a friend because I'm nearer their father's age than theirs. Yet we talk together about their school or work day, and the problems they face. They bring their girlfriends home for meals too!'

# The age gap

Stepfamilies can include a range of ages. The age gap between the couple is often much greater than in first-time relationships – ten to fifteen years is not unusual. So there may almost be two families of children in the stepfamily. The step-parent may have brought up one family, and is now bringing up a second one, and possibly a third if the couple have their own child too.

'The younger of my two sons was eight when my first marriage fell apart. I thought that the hardest childcare work had been completed. But then came a new relationship, remarriage and two young stepdaughters. There are times when I sigh about things like bath night, trips to and from various junior engagements, having to find babysitters, and not being able to go anywhere without travel sickness tablets. But in fact having younger children again has been amazingly positive so far. I feel wiser but not older! I can still almost win the junior school disco dads' dancing competition – my younger stepdaughter couldn't bear the embarrassment, and hid in the toilets, so I must be doing something right!'

Some children will not have had any contact with their father and not know who that is. Others will know who their biological parent is but not have any contact. Others will have a parent who has died. All these situations will have affected the child, and may negatively affect the step-parent/child relationship.

'I thought it would be easy as Daniel's dad had died,' said Andy, 'but it's more complicated than that. Although he doesn't say anything to my face, I sometimes hear him saying that I'm not as good as his dad at cricket or at mending things. It's as though his dad never did anything wrong.'

Being ourselves is part of being a step-parent. Children will soon see through any attempts on our part to be someone we're not. Children learn that no one is perfect, and that both parents and step-parents have their good bits and their not so good bits. As the step-parent of a teenager, it might help to remember words usually attributed to Mark Twain, 'When I was a boy of fourteen, my father was so ignorant I could hardly stand to have the old man around. But when I got to be twenty-one, I was astonished at how much the old man had learned in seven years.'

A rule of thumb suggested by Francesca Adler-Baeder is that it takes as many years as the child's age to reach 'parental status'. 'Parental status is what a child grants us.' With older children, it may not be appropriate to have 'parental status'. Instead the relationship may grow into a healthy one of respect and care.

All these situations will affect the role of the step-parent. So what else defines a step-parent?

## Defining the step-parent

The qualities that make a parent a good parent are the same for a step-parent. It's just that these are practised in a different way. Love, patience, kindness, perseverance, gentleness, goodness and self-control are needed in all parents, and especially in step-parents. As one step-parent expressed it, 'I'm the adult. I have chosen this.'

## Loving through the odds

Loving someone else's child is possible, but it is different from loving one's own children. Because a step-parent was not there at the birth, and is not genetically linked, there isn't that moment when the baby is born and a bond is formed. But love for a stepchild can grow and grow.

Because the English language only has one word for love, it is used to describe all kinds of love: love for parents, love for a friend, love for a sibling, love for a partner, love for a child. There's even love of football, chocolate or shoes. Having different loves doesn't make them less deep or less meaningful, just different. So often step-parents feel guilty because although they love their stepchildren very much, they know that deep down it's not the same as the love they have for their own child.

> 'I love Sam very much, but I know it's not the same as my feelings towards my own children. I think it's that I have an unconditional love for my own children which I don't have for Sam. I'm more willing to forgive them than I am Sam. Don't get me wrong, I would do anything for him. He's a great kid.'

> 'Being a stepmum has been quite a challenge, but I grew to love the girls very much. Then we had a baby of our own. I feel so close to this child and so protective. I didn't know that I could feel this way about another human being. It's been such a struggle not to leave the girls out of everything. I feel guilty that I love my baby more than my lovely stepdaughters.'

When a baby is born, parent and child start on the road to relationship together. In fact the parent will give a lot of love and nurture to the baby before getting a response. Gradually the baby reacts to the parent, smiling and nestling up to them. With stepchildren it will take time to build a relationship and much will have to be invested before showing any returns. This may never develop into love but it can become respect and regard.

## The emotional bank account

It's like opening a bank account. One has to put a lot in before one can draw anything out. Frequently a step-parent has to put a lot into a relationship with a stepchild before seeing any rewards. It often seems that the relationship bank account is not just at zero but starts with a deficit. It can take years and years of input, and there is no guarantee of the size of the payout, but it's still worth it when it happens. As with a bank account, for it to grow there need to be frequent deposits. Even if this has been dormant for a while, deposits can still be made.

## Mutual respect

Respect between stepchild and step-parent is necessary if this stepfamily is to grow. With respect it is possible to work out reasonably amicable arrangements. Without it, so much ends in conflict. Respect has to be earned by the step-parent. It is not a right.

Respect, and possibly love and care, grows when the child sees the actions of the step-parent. How is their own parent treated? How are they treated? What happens when their parent isn't around? The old adage, 'Actions speak louder than words' certainly applies here. Children will watch and make their own judgments!

'In church one Fathers' Day, the minister asked the children to say what was special about their dads. My son was about ten years old and said of his stepdad, "He loves my mum." Since then he has gone on to have a great relationship with his stepdad. In fact people often think they are father and son as they are so alike! They have similar traits like losing their keys, and leaving their mobile phones behind when they leave home.'

## Role models

All parents and step-parents are role models – it's just that some are more helpful models than others. They may give the child an opportunity to see another way of being. A step-parent can provide a positive example of being a man or woman, father or mother. Boys will learn something of being a man from a stepdad. It is said that a girl's first boyfriend is her dad. So a stepdad can compliment her and treat her as a young lady. A stepmum will show femininity to a girl and bring balance to a male household. It's a privilege to be part of the maturing of another person.

> 'I can see the difference in Matthew since he's had Tim as his stepdad. His dad always shouted at him and he was frightened of him. Tim talks to Matthew and explains things. Matthew's much more confident now, and doing better at school.'

## What to call the step-parent

What name a step-parent is called by the child varies too. Younger ones may be happy saying 'Mum' or 'Dad'; others will add the first name – 'Mum Susan' or 'Dad Peter'. Many will use just the step-parent's first name. Some change after time, like Phil's stepson John. Others will change the name after a marriage. And still others have made up a special nickname for their step-parent. Unless the children are very young, accepting what is respectful and the children are comfortable with seems to work best. It's not what the step-parent is called that matters but what kind of person they are and how they relate to the step-child.

> 'Ben calls me, his stepdad, Daddy Richard, and he calls his other dad Daddy Tony. Because he was only four when we got married, it just seemed natural. Tony works away a lot so I'm around much more for Ben. It is confusing for other people to hear Ben talk this way! But it's all very clear to him.'

## A word to stepdads

Traditionally, fathers have been the providers in the family. Although this is not necessarily so, many men still see themselves in that role. Stepdads can make the mistake of seeing themselves as providers and very little else. This would be to miss the richness of relationships. It is important for the couple to discuss what the stepdad's role is, and to be prepared for that to change. It is for the mother to affirm him in this role, and for her to encourage the children to respect him.

## A word to stepmums

Stepmums are still more likely to take on the care of the children – cooking, cleaning and washing, taking to school and activities. It is this aspect of the step-parent role which can cause stress and disagreement. If Stepmum doesn't have children of her own, then this may not be the role she is comfortable with. Others will find their workload has increased as they are looking after more children. Stepmothers find that they are doing much more in the home than they expected, and are surprised by the emotional and physical toll this takes. Many women will be working outside the home too.

> 'We had a week away for our honeymoon, and then I was suddenly mum to two small children. I had dreamed of lazy mornings in bed with my husband – not a chance! I had been a successful career woman, but working out how to meet the demands of a family was so hard.'

'With four of the children needing white shirts for school and Norman a shirt for work each day, there is always ironing to do. Then there's the shopping – my trolley's always overflowing at the check-out. It's a good job I like cooking – teenage boys need constant filling up! As for their bedrooms – well. Sometimes I think my title should be "dogsbody".'

'I was a single mum and I had done well at work and enjoyed being a manager. But nothing had prepared me to run a home, have a husband, and look after my son and two teenagers. I worked out a daily routine, a weekly menu, and a list of chores to be done each day. It was impossible to keep to my plan and to keep everything tidy. The children would be ill, or argumentative, or keep saying they were bored. It was such hard work. I nearly gave up, thinking I wasn't cut out to be a stepmum. It was such a relief to talk to others and learn to be more gentle with myself, and to lower my standards.'

## Children's attachments

When a child is born they start to form attachments to significant adults. Usually this is primarily with the mother, and then with the father, grandparents or carers. If these early relationships have not been satisfactory, then the child may find it difficult to relate to, or attach to, other adults later in life. This may help to explain why some step-parents, and stepmothers in particular, find that their stepchildren are emotionally remote and detached. For a child to be abandoned by its mother is particularly damaging.

Both John Bowlby and his son, Richard, have written extensively about this attachment theory. In Sir Richard Bowlby's view, lack of attachment is significant in stepfamilies but there has been little research into this aspect as yet.

For those stepfamilies where the children live elsewhere but visit, it will take longer for step-relationships to be built.

'We were finding some sort of routine but every now and then things felt blown apart by the arrival of insecure and rather spoilt stepchildren. I resented the way my husband encouraged these step-teens to be dependent and demanding. My husband seemed to father my kids in line with me, but fathered his own totally differently.'

'My step-teens had been parented for years by the time I inherited them and the parenting was not the way I would have done it. I had to learn to loosen up a lot and pick my "battles" carefully. I felt like I was working harder than the step-teens' "real" mum because no matter what happened at least she didn't have to try so hard to love them. I felt bitter at having to give so much whilst only feeling like a very small and unimportant part of their lives. I was trying to kindle a spark of real love, and create a relationship, at a stage not known for its warmth and acceptance of adult authority.

'Now I have real relationships with my step-teens. I enjoy their company and I know that I've been a valuable part of their growing up.'

## Children at home or away

Some step-parents may have children of their own who don't live with them but who visit them, whilst others may have children with whom they have no contact. Living with someone else's children can be painful, as they can be a daily reminder of those other children. It's right to acknowledge the hurt. Denying it won't make it go away. But that pain, and perhaps anger too, mustn't be transferred to the children who are living in the family. They are not to blame.

There are lots of ways to let children know they are still thought about. Postcards are an excellent and inexpensive way to keep in touch and can be sent from places visited, or chosen because the picture has particular relevance to the child. Agreeing to watch the same TV programme to be discussed later by phone is another approach. With the growth of the Internet, emails and webcams are quick and cheap ways to communicate.

Memory boxes are a way of storing up memories to share one day with a child when there is no contact. Collect photos, tickets and souvenirs and perhaps one day it will be possible to share them with the child. This will help to 'fill in the gaps' since the last meeting, and will also show the child that they were not forgotten.

## Getting to know each other

If the step-parent has not been a parent before, or if the stepchildren are older than the step-parent's children, it is very important to know something about the development of children and teenagers. Much conflict arises because the step-parent expects more mature behaviour and more thoughtfulness than the child is able to give. Reading about child development, talking to other parents of similar aged children or attending parenting courses will give a better understanding of what is regarded as normal behaviour. For example: teenagers do need lots of sleep – they aren't just being lazy. Recent research suggests that because brains aren't fully developed it is physically difficult for them to be more considerate and less self-centred.

Consider how much the stepchildren know about their step-parent. They may know something of the person they are living with, but what of their early years, schooling and hobbies? Sharing some of the step-parent's history will help in building a relationship.

As the child grows, so more age-appropriate stories can be told. This can start quite simply with how did the step-parent get their name, did they like school, what was their favourite subject, which subject did they hate, what games did they play. Draw a timeline with the key events in the step-parent's life marked on it. The parent could join in as children are often curious about their parent's life too. Laugh together over old photos.

## Humour and silence

It is sometimes wise to remain silent and a sense of humour will really help in lots of situations:

> 'I can still taste that cup of tea seemingly kindly made for me by my future stepdaughter – who then deliberately substituted salt for sugar! I took a sip, realized what the little angel had done, and managed to show no reaction. However, she was unable to hide her disappointment. She had wanted to make me look an idiot in front of a group of people she sensed I was ill at ease with. They were other members of her family who were showing open hostility to me.
>
> 'I didn't even mention this event to her father until quite some time afterwards when we were both able to have a good laugh about it, as indeed have my stepdaughter and I done since then.'

## Rise to the challenge

Step-parenting is a challenge. It can also be an opportunity to have a close relationship with a child, and to be part of that child's development and life. It can be a very satisfying and significant role.

'The best thing about being a stepdad isn't unique to being a stepdad. I think all fathers feel like this. When the kids do something amazing there's such a pride inside. You think "That's my kid out there!" and you prod the person next to you and say, "That's my son", "that's my daughter!" Sometimes it can be quite hard to know that you're not their "real" dad. It would have been great to be around them when they were younger, but on the other hand you have to say, "but I am their father now". It's about dealing with the past and looking forward to the future and saying, "I will be a father if you want me to."'

## To Think About

- How do you define your role as Stepmum or Stepdad?
- How do you feel about not being the child's biological mum or dad?
- How do you think the children see you?
- How would you like them to see you?

# CHAPTER 7

# Parenting steps

Parenting in a stepfamily involves both the biological parent and the step-parent. This is a team effort, with both sharing the load, but with different responsibilities. For this type of parenting there needs to be co-operation, communication and flexibility.

## The biological parent

If the step-parent is to have a significant role in the life of the child, then the biological parent is the one who will enable this to happen. How this parent sees the role of the step-parent is crucial. Their view will govern how much they will allow the step-parent to be involved in the life of the child.

The biological parent may have been parenting alone for some time. They will be used to setting the rules, and following their own way of parenting. Many such parents are very protective of their children. They have been used to doing most or all of the parenting. They don't want to see their child hurt further in any way. There may have been many pressures, emotionally, physically and mentally, and they may have had little energy left to correct their child. They may have made a conscious effort to parent differently from the other biological parent. Some parents will have tried to compensate for the situation they are now in and have indulged the child, especially if they were the parent to end the previous relationship and feel guilty about this. Other parents may have treated the child as the other adult in the family, giving them responsibility and sharing with them emotionally as though they were equals. After the death of a parent, other people too may have said to the child, 'Well, you're the man (or woman) of the house now.' Many single parents have a very close relationship with their child.

## The step-parent

The step-parent will be stepping into this parent/child relationship. It is a wise person who will step cautiously and carefully into it, waiting to be welcomed rather than assuming a right to be there. The biological parent is wise to encourage the step-parent to take their place gradually.

'I watched Tim with my children. I wanted to know how he would treat them. I would be trusting him with them if he became their stepdad. They are the most precious things in my life. At first, I didn't like it when Tim corrected them. I didn't want them to be hurt or frightened again. I knew that if we were going to be a family, then Tim had to have a parenting role. It's taken me a long time to really trust Tim and sometimes to let him deal with a situation and set the boundaries. We have lots of chats about parenting.'

Phil says that he and Vicky have talked a lot about bringing up John. 'When I look after John, and Vicky isn't there, I try to parent in the way I know she would want. So I try to follow her rules and let John do as she would let him do. I don't always agree with her but after all he is her son.'

## Primary and secondary parenting

One way to look at parenting in a stepfamily is to see the biological parent as the primary parent and the step-parent as the secondary parent. Thus the biological parent takes the lead, and is more often the one to set the boundaries and give correction. The step-parent follows this lead, backing up the parent and taking responsibility when necessary.

It is similar to the difference between parenting and grand-parenting. Usually parents are the prime carers, parenting the way they consider is best. When the child stays with grandparents, wise grandparents will seek to follow this style as much as possible but will act 'in loco parentis' if necessary. The key difference in a stepfamily is that the parenting style should be discussed and some agreement reached between the biological parent and the step-parent. It is then for the biological parent to explain any changes to the child.

'We had very similar parenting styles, so we generally agreed how to treat the children. However, there were some things that had to change as a result of having more children in the house,' says Jill. 'Norman's boys were used to raiding the fridge when they came home from school. I would go to cook dinner and find half the ingredients that I wanted and had bought earlier had disappeared! We changed that practice so that they didn't start on new packets of food without asking. Then Norman explained to the boys that some of their videos were not suitable to be left in the lounge with younger children around now. They were OK about it once they understood why things had to change.'

## Different parenting styles

More difficulty arises if the parenting styles are different. There is a tendency for everyone to think that their view of parenting is the right one. If each one holds on to this, there will be no room for manoeuvre. Even quite small differences can become contentious. For example: Should the child sit at a table to eat, or sit on the floor watching television? Should there be a time for bed every night, or should this move according to circumstances? Can the child walk to the shop alone or not? How a person was parented will also influence how they choose to parent. So if they had to do chores around the house they may expect the child to do so as well. Others will have resented doing chores as a child and won't want the child to help at all.

Parenting styles range from the strict, disciplinarian, authoritarian approach through to the lax, nonconformist, unstructured form. If the biological parent and the step-parent's styles are nearer to one approach or the other, they will be able to resolve any differences quite easily. But if, for example, the biological parent is very authoritarian and the step-parent is very permissive, there will be conflict over the way the child is parented. It will need a willingness on the part of both adults to see parenting styles as neither right nor wrong, and a determination to find the middle ground for the benefit of everyone. This middle way allows for rules and routines, but with incentives and consequences that are known to everyone. When the child is older, they are included in discussion and negotiation.

It takes courage and a lot of honest discussion to talk about parenting in this way. Emotional blackmail and negative attitudes have to stop. Saying things like: 'They're *my* children. *You* don't understand,' or *'You're* too soft. They need to grow up, I'll knock them into shape' will only add to the conflict.

> **Susan and Peter soon discovered that they parented in very different ways. Peter had been to boarding school and then joined the army. He had a list of rules which he expected his daughter to obey without question. He expected everything and everyone to be neat and tidy. 'But I believe that children need to be independent, making their own decisions, and to learn from their own mistakes. I am more laid back and encourage individuality,' Susan explains. 'We tried to continue to use our own styles, disrespecting each other and confusing the children. We've had lots of rows over this, and it has nearly destroyed our family. Now we're getting help from a counsellor to understand why we feel so strongly about our ways, and to help us to work together instead of pulling apart.'**

## A child's view

Disagreement between the parent and step-parent may be used by the child to their advantage! All children will seek out the parent from whom they think they are more likely to get what they want. If they see their parent as the ally, and the parent always takes their side, then a deep wedge will be driven between the child and the step-parent, and ultimately between the parent and step-parent. It won't have the same effect the other way round. If the child sees an ally in their step-parent, this will tend to strengthen their relationship and not damage the parent/child one either. As in all families, a united front by the parents is the best one. This might mean checking sometimes before agreeing to a particular course of action.

'It didn't matter how small my request was, Ruth and Rebecca were always told that they didn't have to do it. So if I asked them to hang up their coats or take off their muddy shoes they ignored me. My opinions didn't matter. Ruth complained that I made her eat food she didn't like. But her mother let her eat a lot of trash food. I was definitely the bad guy and Mum was the saviour. I felt that neither the girls nor their mother respected me. Eventually I left.'

John soon learned that his stepdad loved animals. He really wanted a dog, but Mum would have none of it. John would often talk about dogs with Phil who had had one as a child. John and Phil 'ganged up' together to ask Vicky to consider having a family dog. Vicky knew what was happening and having a dog became a frequent family topic. 'Eventually I agreed,' says Vicky, laughing, 'and we went to choose the puppy together. Now I'm the one who spoils the dog and buys treats for him!'

A step-parent has to walk the delicate balance between having a part in the parenting of the child and yet not having the legal or moral right to dictate how the child is brought up.

## Values systems

Parenting is also based on people's values and beliefs. If the couple share the same or similar views about the meaning of life, and what is good or evil, then they will have a common foundation for parenting. If their core beliefs are very different, then this will add to their differences in parenting. Those with a strong religious faith will instruct their children about it, and while they are young, expect them to follow this teaching. This may include observing festivals and rituals, wearing certain clothes and following a particular diet. Others may be more agnostic, and less directive about what they teach their children. Parents in any family may come from different social, economic and cultural backgrounds, but in a stepfamily these differences can add to the struggle to parent together. Discussion and flexibility are the only ways forward.

## Discipline of children

Dr Francesca Adler-Baeder, an educator and researcher in the field of child development and family science, states that 'A strict, authoritarian approach to discipline on the part of the step-parent will not aid the relationship. The child is legally right when they say, "You're not my parent. You can't make me do … ."' Some people see their authority over a child as being their right because they are the adult: 'Because I say so.' They expect the child to obey. Thus the parent or step-parent insists on having the control. Such an approach to discipline relies on ordering, punishing and threatening. Many people will have been parented this way. But this more bombastic and less considered stance, especially if carried out by the step-parent, is likely to alienate the child.

'Clean shoes for church were so important. If they were dirty she went ballistic. Rules were presented to us as being the way to live,' says Wendy of her stepmother. 'She worked full-time as a teacher and reasoned that she knew what to do with my sister and myself. Knowing about child development is not the same as parenting! She ran our home like a boot camp. She just didn't seem to care how scared I was about walking home from Brownies in the dark on my own. As a teenager I was anorexic and I wanted to die. My sister ran away from home after being expelled from school.'

However, it is right that there are rules and boundaries in the stepfamily home and that the step-parent and parent should make these together.

Many parents and step-parents see discipline as a major difficulty in stepfamilies. Discipline is often thought of as punishment for the child who disobeys. If discipline is seen much more as the whole way a child learns, so that it includes praise and affirmation as well as correction, it will make it easier to resolve. The Latin root for discipline is *disciplina* meaning instruction, teaching, training and education. So working out what the adults want the child to learn is the starting point. Asking questions that begin with 'Why do we want... to behave in this way, put away his things, clear the table, do his homework' will help to determine whether they are for the child's good or the parent's convenience. It's amazing how many things a child is expected to do are for the parent's benefit! This doesn't make them wrong, but enables the parents to decide which behaviours they want to encourage and why.

Children, and adults too, often respond to what is expected of them. (In any meeting, if the speaker asks the audience to stand, raise their hand or turn off their mobile phone, this is almost universally obeyed!) If children are expected to behave in the approved manner, they generally will. If no one expects them to do as they are asked, then they generally won't. So, one aspect of discipline is expectation. If the parent and/or step-parent are waiting for the child to be disobedient, they probably will be.

Of course, children need boundaries. Some of these are necessary for life: Don't play with fire, don't run out into the road, don't walk along the railway track. Other boundaries make for pleasant relationships: saying please and thank you, holding the door open for the next person, not spitting at someone. Other boundaries are family ones: not going into anyone's bedroom without knocking first, waiting till everyone is served before eating, doing household chores, walking the dog. The stepfamily's shape will depend on the boundaries that are set for it. These may include some from the previous family and some that are new. If these boundaries are explained to the children, they will find it easier to accept them, even when they are different from their past experiences or the boundaries that are kept in their other parent's home. Boundaries need to be reconsidered from time to time as the children get older. Some may no longer be suitable, and others may be necessary. All children push against the boundaries some of the time – some more than others.

Deciding what punishment fits the crime is another topic for the parent and step-parent to seek agreement on. Time out is one popular way to restrict a younger child. When the child misbehaves, they are required to sit on either a 'naughty' stair or a particular chair for one minute for each year of their life. So a four-year-old would sit on the chair for four minutes. Older children might be 'grounded' and have to stay in when they would rather be with their friends. Withholding pocket money is another well-used practice. Discussing with the child what punishment they think is fair for breaking the rules is often surprising. They tend to be more severe than the parents are! It is most important that the consequences of wrong actions are explained in advance to the child, and that these are carried out every time. Again it works best, especially in the early years of the stepfamily, if the parent is the one to explain any new rules and is usually the one to impose any punishment. No one copes well with lots of changes all at once. New family ways can be introduced slowly. All the children in the family, whether resident or visiting, should be expected to follow the same family rules and to receive the same age-appropriate correction.

## Circle time

It may be helpful to have family meetings, or 'circle time', so that everyone can have their say and have their issues looked at together. This works best with primary age children. Take it in turns to choose one topic for discussion for each meeting. The rules are that everyone has the opportunity to speak, while the others listen and don't interrupt, tease or criticize. The use of an egg timer will limit the length of time one person speaks! The aim is to find a way forward that will work for this family.

## Resident and visiting children

It can be tempting to treat visiting children differently, allowing them more latitude because the parent has less time with them. This doesn't help the child to integrate with other family members, or to feel part of this family if they are always treated like a guest. Resident children will resent any favouritism and may transfer this resentment onto the visiting children and their parent. If there are reasons to treat a child differently, these should to be shared with all the children. For example: one child may have additional needs, requiring extra physical help and understanding.

It is difficult when parent and step-parent have different ideas about what behaviour is acceptable and what is not, and about what punishments are appropriate. However, if the child doesn't like the step-parent's correction, and the parent doesn't support the step-parent, the child is most likely to retort, 'You are not my parent. I don't have to do what you say.' Since step-parents are in a less secure position with their stepchildren, and may not be sure of their role as a step-parent, this situation will undermine them. Their reaction will be either flight or fight. Flight may be literal (they leave the family), or it may be emotional, distancing themselves from interacting with the child and/or with their partner. Fight may not be physical, but consist of verbal and emotional attacks. Very quickly people become entrenched in their view points, and change becomes harder. A mediator or counsellor may be needed to help the couple resolve their conflict if their stepfamily is to survive and mature.

## Building bridges

It isn't always easy for step-parents to tell a stepchild directly how much they love and care about them. It's great if they can, but their own reservations and family background might mean that they and the child find face-to-face expressions awkward and embarrassing. Writing little notes and leaving them on the child's pillow or sending appropriate cards are also ways to say how much the child is valued. Such gestures might not be immediately acknowledged, but they can be building bricks in the relationship. Physical touch is important, but should be offered with care. Some children are more touchy-feely than others. Be guided by what the child wants and follow their lead. Everyone should feel comfortable about physical contact.

All children and stepchildren need consistency, loving care and boundaries if they are to flourish. These are possible in a stepfamily if the parent and step-parent work at finding a parenting structure that they can both adhere to. A sense of humour helps too:

'In my first marriage I had become accustomed to an obsessively tidy home. When I married Annette and we became a stepfamily, I would find the rooms strewn with children's toys, which frustrated me so I became determined "to teach these kids how to be tidy". My master strategy was to put the toys in black plastic sacks and throw them onto the back lawn. I imagined my stepchildren would soon learn I wasn't a person to be messed with. Wrong! In fact, they treated the whole thing as a bit of a lark and continued to be as untidy as ever.

'The drama came to a head after I returned late one night from a trip away. Everyone was asleep. Rather than risk waking them up, I undressed downstairs, left my clothes folded on the settee and crept up into bed. When I arose next morning and went down for my clothes, they had disappeared. Yes, there they were in a black sack on the back lawn. I turned to see three little faces poking around the edge of the door warily checking my reaction. They soon joined me in roaring laughter as I realized in a flash I'd got my comeuppance and that I was the one who needed to adapt, not them.'

## To Think About

• Consider your response to the following scenarios. Are they the same or different to your partner's answers?

1. **The five-year-old refuses to eat his dinner. Would you:**
   a) offer him something he likes
   b) ignore him, and let him wait till the next meal for more food
   c) insist he remains seated until he has finished the meal

2. **The twelve-year-old hasn't done his homework and it's 9 p.m. Would you:**
   a) help him to complete it immediately
   b) shrug, and leave him to face the consequences
   c) tell him that he'll never succeed, insist that he goes to his room and completes all the work immediately

3. **The fourteen-year-old is still in bed at 7.30 a.m. and the school bus leaves at 8.00 a.m. Would you:**
   a) **possibly make yourself late for work by dropping him off at school on your way to work if he isn't ready for the bus**
   b) **remind him once of the time, then leave the house as planned**
   c) **shout at him every five minutes that he'll have to walk, and then go and drag him out of bed**

4. **Two of the children are fighting again. Would you:**
   a) **plead with them to stop, and offer a treat as a reward for stopping**
   b) **leave them to sort out their disagreement themselves unless one is being hurt**
   c) **threaten punishment if they don't stop immediately**

If you answered mostly 'a', then your parenting style is permissive.
If you answered mostly 'b', then your parenting style is more in the middle – often referred to as democratic.
If you answered mostly 'c', then your parenting style is authoritarian.

• Discuss with your partner any different replies that you gave. How will you find a way forward to parent together?

# CHAPTER 8

# Steps in the step-parent/ step-child relationship

New relationships often follow a similar pattern, and these can be used as the basis for those in a stepfamily. They start with a wary 'who are you?' step. Both parties will reveal a little about themselves to see what reaction they get. They will often be 'on their best behaviour' towards each other. Some relationships, which are best described as acquaintances, don't progress beyond this stage.

Step two happens when people pass the 'we're careful to find areas in common' stage into areas of differences. Here the surface relationship may look OK, but underneath concerns and frustrations creep in. As these undercurrents grow the relationship is threatened. Those involved may decide to do nothing at all, or fight their corner on every issue so that they become enemies.

If the relationship is to develop, then each one will need to decide which areas are not important to agree on, which areas to follow the approach of the other person, and which areas need to be discussed until a resolution can be found.

As knowledge and understanding grow, there is a shape to this relationship which makes it unique. Shared thoughts and activities allow it to deepen. There is still some uncertainty about its strength and ability to last.

The final step occurs when the relationship is secure. There is a sense of loyalty to each other and an attachment. Both parties believe it will weather any storms and will last.

In the step-parent/stepchild relationship there is also a pattern. Many step-parents and stepchildren start at step one. The first meeting goes OK, and subsequent ones suggest that all is well. Everyone involved makes an effort to get on. The step-parent wants to make a good impression, especially on their new partner. The child may be delighted by the attention of another adult. It's easy to jump to the conclusion that this good start will continue. It may not!

Others start with very hostile reactions from the child. Living together and marriage are not going to change this. It's going to take a lot of work, patience and understanding on the part of the step-parent for any change in attitude, and it may never happen. Considering why the child is behaving in this way may show how to approach this relationship.

Whenever someone is attacked, either verbally or physically, the natural reactions are to fight or flee. Whilst this is a good instinct when faced with wild animals, it doesn't help to build relationships! When a stepchild shouts, 'I hate you' it doesn't help to shout back, 'I hate you too.' Nor does it help to retreat with 'If that's the way you feel that's OK by me' and to refuse to have any more contact than necessary, or no contact at all.

To turn the other cheek, and reply with 'I'm sorry you feel that way. I would like us to be friends' is not easy. But if this relationship is to succeed, then it is for the step-parent to lead the way.

There will be things about the child that the step-parent doesn't like. It's true in all relationships! It isn't possible to alter all of these, and it's wise not to try to change most of them. Decide which aspect is most unacceptable and discuss this very carefully with the child's biological parent. Most parents are very protective of their children, and react defensively to any real or perceived criticism. It helps to start with 'I find it difficult when...' rather than 'Your child...'.

## Moving forward

Both stepchild and step-parent are finding their way in this relationship. Certainly the child will have had experiences which influence their attitude to their step-parent. Continuing time and effort by the step-parent is required, probably for years and years, if this bond is to reach the final step.

Talking of her relationship with her stepson, Adam, Alice says, 'He was never openly hostile to me, just indifferent. He didn't live with us but often visited. He was polite but very distant. It was hard to find common ground. Adam was in the Sea Cadets and I attended their display evening with his father. That was a start and I felt more accepted. Over the years it got better. My daughter was bridesmaid at his wedding. I've just received at letter from him which ended "We will always be there for you. You can count on our love and support for the rest of your life."'

Here are some ways to build a positive step-parent/child relationship:

• Spend time doing things together as a family – outings, holidays, celebrations, watching and discussing TV, doing household chores.

- Spend time together – sharing a hobby, taking the dog for a walk, going to a football match, buying a present for Mum or Dad, working together, learning from each other.
- Share personal stories – about childhood, school and work.
- Take an interest in whatever the child is interested in. Don't try to be very keen about something when not, as the child will spot this a mile off. But learn enough about it to have a conversation and to ask appropriate questions.
- Have fun together.
- Show that you care. Words are important but they are not enough. Actions speak louder than words.
- Keep your mouth shut on many occasions! Don't criticize and don't moan all the time.
- Develop a thick enough skin not to take everything personally.
- Learn more about child development and parenting through books, TV programmes, parenting courses and talking to other parents.
- Aim to be a 'good enough' step-parent.
- Be prepared for the long haul.

'Soon after we married, we got a family dog. We all suggested names for her. We discarded those we couldn't imagine calling out at the park! Then I found that it was easier to chat to my stepson when we went for long walks with the dog. Somehow it was less threatening to be walking alongside each other than to face each other head on. We started with safe things like cricket and football but now we'll chat about anything.'

## Expressions of love

Gary Chapman, in his book, *The Five Love Languages*, describes five ways of giving and receiving love. They are:

1. **Words of Affirmation – saying nice things, praise and compliments.**
2. **Acts of Service – doing thoughtful things for the other person.**
3. **Gifts – thoughtful presents rather than expensive ones.**
4. **Quality Time – spending good time with the person, concentrating on them.**
5. **Touch – physical touch, age and relationship appropriate.**

People tend to have one or two of these which are most important to them to receive so that they feel loved and cared about. Children are just the same. Finding out which of these matters to the stepchild will help the step-parent to focus on the ways that make the child feel most cared about. In fact all five are good steps in this relationship.

## Don't give up!

Many step-parents come to love their stepchildren, and do have very positive relationships with them. For the child this may be even better than the one they have with their biological parent. However, a step-parent will never be the same as the biological parent.

Tony Parsons, in his book *Man and Boy*, says, 'Without ever really trying to match him, I knew that I could never mean as much in Peggy's life as he did. That's what hurt most of all... he would always be her father.'

Perhaps the motto of a step-parent should be 'Don't give up!' The rewards may be a long time coming. Being a step-parent is a choice.

Mark sums this up:

'I have found that as a step-parent one has the opportunity to have all the challenging things of parenthood and all the good. I am both a stepson and a stepfather. I can only be the stepfather that I am because of the example of my stepfather. I can only be a father because someone chose to be a father to me.'

## To Think About

- Consider your relationship with each stepchild. What can you do to encourage this relationship to develop further, or change if you're not satisfied with it as it is?
- In what ways do you show each child that you care about them?
- What are the ways that each child in the family receives love?

# Family steps – children

# CHAPTER 9

# Children's steps

Every child who becomes a stepchild has suffered loss. For whatever reason, this child is not living with both biological parents. Even when the child has no knowledge of their missing father, they are still aware of the loss. They have a genetic link to both parents. Many adults, especially adoptees, will search for information about their unknown biological parents. The loss is more apparent if the child has been living with both parents.

Linda Goldman, a grief therapist and author, writes 'Children naturally assume their world will be filled with safety, kindness, and meaning as they attempt to answer the universal questions of who am I and why am I here.' When this 'world' is turned upside down, children are hurt and confused.

Bereavement due to death or divorce follows a similar emotional pattern. Elisabeth Kübler-Ross, a world authority on death recognized five stages of dying which have generally been accepted as the five stages of grieving for a loved one: denial, anger, bargaining, depression and acceptance. In the book, *All Alone* by Jill Worth and Christine Tufnell, the single-parent journey is described in similar terms.

Some of the characteristics of children's grief are dependent on their age and emotional development. They may have physical symptoms such as headaches and stomach aches, or regressive behaviour such as bed-wetting or thumb-sucking. Their anger may be directed at the one who has left, at God, or transferred to the remaining parent or incoming step-parent. Children often feel guilty and somehow responsible for what has happened, even though that may seem illogical to the adults affected. They tend to fear the future: What if the remaining parent dies or leaves? They may worry about the parent who is now alone. Children often seem OK for periods of time and then very upset at other times. Grief can be like the waves of the sea, gentle and rippling or crashing in over the rocks.

> Leanne is now in her forties. She is just coming to recognize that her mother's suicide when Leanne was twelve was not her fault. 'I had gone into the lounge still wearing my muddy boots. I can see the dirt on the carpet now. The next thing I remember is being told that my mother had died and being sent to my room. As I was often in trouble, I thought that I had been really bad this time and that that was why my mother had died.'

> 'I thought maybe I didn't make him enough cups of coffee. Would he have stayed if I did? What if I had eaten all of my dinner instead of pushing it all to the side of the plate? Would he have stayed then?' Louise is ten. 'What can a ten-year-old do to make their dad stay with them? ... Not a lot, it seems.'

Just like adults, children need time and support to work through their loss. They may not have the vocabulary to express their feelings. It's rather like an adult trying to draw anger – some will depict a scene with stick men, others will use colour, and still others will stare at a blank piece of paper and not know where to begin. The child's grief may be complicated by sudden or traumatic events: murder, suicide, abduction. Professional help may be needed. They will not 'get over it' but can find a 'new normal'.

In addition to the loss of a parent, the child may have had to move home, change locality, school, clubs or church and no longer have contact with the same friends and family. These are additional losses and changes which can add to the child's insecurity and frustration.

> 'It was a shock when my dad left us. I couldn't understand what was happening. My mum was very upset and we spent a lot of time with my grandparents. I only told my best friend at school. I told my mum, "If Dad had loved me he wouldn't have left me." Dad told me that Mum made him ill. I talked to Mum and Granny, but my younger brother bottled it all up. Three years later, when Mum met my stepdad, I was very wary of him.'

Into the life of a grieving child comes the step-parent. If they see the step-parent as the reason why their parents are still not together, they will resent this person. If they think that the step-parent's presence means they have to forget the dead parent or the one they no longer live with, they may be bitter. If the child has been able to work through some of their losses, they will be more able to relate to a step-parent.

## The present effect on the step-child

The stepfamily spells out to the child that their dream of having both parents living together is over. The child may try to break this couple relationship, believing that if the step-parent leaves their parent will return to the other parent. This may account for some of the child's aggressive and disruptive behaviour.

> 'I set out to make him hate me and leave. I thought we'd be better off without him. I blamed my stepdad for everything. I didn't think about how my mum might be feeling. I was so hurt and angry. I was obnoxious. Amazingly he stayed. Now we get on OK.'

Either or both parents may have had a number of partners, and so the child may have experienced other step-parents too. These changes will add to the child's concerns that this stepfamily may not last either. How does the child know that this step-parent is going to stay? If they get close to their step-parent, they might get hurt again if the step-parent leaves. It's not surprising that children often keep their step-parents at an emotional arm's length away.

Louise says, 'So Dad had someone else and she didn't like kids. That was another thing I couldn't understand. Why do you want to be with a woman who doesn't like the fact that you've got three kids? Their marriage only lasted eighteen months. We were in the car when Dad told me he was seeing someone new. My heart sank. I didn't want to meet someone else, if they were just going to walk in and out of my life again. I wanted someone stable, someone who will stick around.'

David was eleven when Dad finally left home. 'Mum went on to have a number of male friends, and some treated me badly, and then Pete arrived. He had long hair, wore ragged jeans and spoke in the local accent. He definitely wasn't into keeping up appearances and social climbing. He is such a contrast to Dad, who is a business man with a position to maintain. During my teenage years I remember we played pool, cricket and cards together. He didn't say much but these were formative years. Pete gave me male attention in a reasonably secure family unit.'

It will take considerable time for a stepchild to come to trust that this step-parent is for them and is going to stay in partnership with their parent. Both parent and step-parent will have to prove this by actions as well as words.

'Why should I trust my stepmum? If my natural mother would rather live with someone else, why should this woman care about me? She's OK and we get on alright but I miss my mum. Mum lives with Martin but he doesn't like me, so I only see Mum when he's out.'

## Change – positives and negatives

Change is a natural part of life, but is often resisted. Change can be felt as either a positive thing or a negative one. Children changing from primary to secondary school can find that an exciting challenge or daunting and scary. It is easier to manage change if there is preparation and understanding. Similarly, living in a stepfamily, with all the changes that take place, can be seen in a more positive light with a little forethought and imagination. It helps if the child is prepared and able to share in some of the discussions, especially about areas that affect them.

'We liked the idea that Jill, our stepmum, would be living with us as she is a much better cook than Dad! It's nice that when we get home from school she is there. She cooks great cakes. She's a bit strict and wants to know if we're going to be late in, but Dad says that's because she cares about us.'

'We had visited our stepdad's house lots of times before we moved in so we knew what it was like. It was much better than where we lived before – my brother and I now have a big bedroom and don't have to have bunk beds anymore. We still go to the same school but it takes us longer to get there. We can play football and cricket in the garden.'

'When my mum met my stepdad she never really told me and my brother they were going out until they were engaged. At that point he started staying over at the house, albeit on the sofa, but we felt he was an intruder in our home. They never sat us down to talk about anything. Consequently when they got married and he started trying to act as the man of the house it caused a lot of friction.

'I left home and very rarely visit them. My brother stayed and suffered quite a lot. He withdrew into himself to avoid the conflict. He eventually left without anywhere to go and is currently in a hostel for homeless people.'

## The child's feelings

Being a stepchild often means having more grown-ups involved in your life. It is possible for the child to have two parents and two current step-parents plus a whole heap of other relations. It can seem to the child that their life is being controlled by a lot of people, without any recourse to their wishes. Of course, children can't have life as they want it all the time, but they can have their feelings about things considered. Including them in discussions about holidays, interior decorating, buying a new TV or moving house will help them to feel part of the family. It will also equip them to make considered choices when they are older.

The parent will have a different bond to their own children to that which they have with their stepchildren. It is the parent and step-parent's responsibility to see that they treat all the children in a similar way as far as possible.

## Building up the new family

Stepfamilies can bring together two sets of children – his and hers. Some or all of these children may live all the time, some of the time or never in the stepfamily. Mixing children adds to the complexity of stepfamily life! Just like siblings, stepsiblings can relate well some of the time and argue at other times. They have to build their own relationships with their stepsiblings.

Parents can provide opportunities for this to happen and minimize potential areas of conflict:

- If the stepsiblings have to share bedrooms, how can these be arranged so that everyone has a little bit of space that is their own?
- What are the rules about privacy, and asking before borrowing personal possessions?
- Do the same rules and boundaries apply to all the children?
- Do the children think they are treated fairly? How could this be resolved?
- Are they able to continue with their hobbies and friends?
- Are similar amounts of money spent on each one for presents and treats? Amounts spent on clothes and other personal items may be different according to age.
- Can you plan family fun times together?

'We stayed in our own bedrooms when our stepsiblings came to live with us so that was OK. We carried on much as normal. It is strange having younger ones around but it's nice that they look up to us. They have to do the same jobs in the house as us. Me and my brother usually wash up the saucepans and they do the plates and knives and forks.'

'I like to go to my room and do my own thing. It's what I'm used to. My stepbrother and stepsister are always arguing. I like having someone to play with on the PlayStation. I have to share things more. We all go camping, which I like.'

# Birth order

There has been much research about the effects of birth order in the family on personality. Whilst the specific details vary, it does seem that the eldest is a natural leader, perfectionist and conformist, that the middle child is a peacemaker and often has the least number of photos in the family album, and that the youngest is an extrovert who likes getting their own way. An only child tends to be well organized, conscientious and dependable, but doesn't accept criticism very well.

If living in a stepfamily changes this order, then the child may be confused and show this in their behaviour. For an only child, sharing and the general rough and tumble of siblings is strange. They have not had to fight to get attention, and haven't learned how to handle teasing and to have sibling arguments. Other children may now be in a different place – a youngest becomes a middle and may not receive all the attention as the baby of the family, whilst an eldest is now further down the line and has lost his or her privileged position.

The parent and step-parent can be aware of any changes and the possible effects on each child. They can compensate for this where appropriate and help the children to adjust to their current positions. For example: giving extra attention to a youngest who is now a middle; allowing an only to have space away from the family.

Most people have an inborn sense of justice and fairness. Children often say, 'It isn't fair.' Asking the child about this will help the parent to decide what they should do about it. There are times when life isn't fair. However, the child may have a grievance which can be solved. Much stepsibling rivalry stems from insecurity, perceived favouritism and jealousy. Looking at what is behind the rivalry will help to determine what action is suitable.

## Challenging behaviour

Children misbehave for a reason! This may seem to be because they are stubborn and disobedient children, but children's behaviour says something about them and their needs. There is a need in everyone to belong to a group, to feel loved, wanted and valued. Many times children misbehave to get attention. Bad attention is better than none! When the parents and step-parents are caught up in their own emotions and practical pressures, the child can feel left out. This can be clearly seen when two adults meet out shopping and stop to talk. The child is ignored so starts to play around. If this behaviour goes unnoticed, they will develop more unacceptable play, until someone shouts at them!

## Making adjustments

Children in a stepfamily can feel ignored when there are other siblings and stepsiblings, and the parent and step-parent are trying to develop their couple relationship. Children may have been used to the undivided attention of their parent when they lived in a single-parent family. Now they have to share their parent, and it will take time for them to adjust. Reassurance and special one-to-one times with that parent will help them to accept the new situation.

It may be that the child doesn't have the attention, or feel valued and loved, by their other parent. They might seek to have this need met by demanding more attention from the one parent and from their step-parent. As the child feels more secure in the care of these adults, they will gradually be less demanding.

## Praise!

It's important with all children to find as many opportunities as possible to praise them – for good behaviour, for trying hard, for caring, for being the person that they are. Focusing on all the good will give them the attention they need without them resorting to behaviour that is not approved of.

## Choices within boundaries

Sometimes children seem determined to win at all costs! Then the parent or step-parent joins the battle, neither wanting to give in and lose. The child may have been used to having quite a lot of independence and power in their former family. Understandably they don't want to give this up just because they are in a stepfamily. Giving children choices within boundaries will give such a child the opportunity to have some say and independence. So offering several alternatives will avoid a win/lose situation arising. For example: choosing when and where they will do their homework, choosing which one from a list of chores they will do each day, choosing buying their clothes within a given price range. They may also respond well to family discussions about rules and consequences, and will need to understand the reasons for them.

## The hurting child

When anyone feels hurt, the natural response is to hurt back – wanting revenge. Children in a stepfamily have been hurt. They are not living with both parents. They may have learned to accept this and are quite content. Others will still be hurting inside, and be angry about all that has happened. They may also be hurt and angry about living in the stepfamily. Children often don't have the vocabulary to express their feelings in words or the maturity to resolve them, so they act out their emotions in the way they behave. This may be by being defiant, deliberately breaking rules, or destroying property. The parent feels very hurt and can't understand why their child is acting in this way, and the step-parent questions whether they can live with such a child.

Again, praising the child whenever possible is important. Hate the behaviour, not the child. Encourage the child to talk, and be prepared to listen without jumping to conclusions or immediately defending the adults. Children may prefer to talk to someone outside the family, and may need professional help. Giving them the names of a number of appropriate people and organizations means they can choose whom they want to talk to. They may feel they can't talk about their parents and other family members outside the home because of disloyalty or fear of retribution. It helps to give the child permission to talk about family matters with someone else.

## The withdrawn child

Children, and adults too, can feel that they are failures, and that anything they try to do always fails as well. As children sometimes blame themselves for the breakdown in their parents' relationship, they also fear being the reason this current couple relationship doesn't last either. Rather than add to what is going on in the stepfamily, they withdraw. They refuse to try to do anything, fearing making mistakes and getting into trouble. This lack of self-esteem limits them and the family. It is important for this child to succeed. It doesn't matter how small the task, the child needs to achieve it. It is also important for this child, and all the family, to learn that mistakes and accidents happen, but that doesn't make them failures.

## The blame game

When one child's behaviour is particularly challenging, they may become the focus and get blamed for all the difficulties in the stepfamily. 'If (name) was different, we'd be OK.' Rather than look for things in the adults which might need changing, they ignore these and see all the problems as being the fault of this child. This child is a member of the family, and is not responsible for all the struggles. It is for the adults to find ways, and possibly outside help too, to enable this child to have a less destructive place in the family.

'Perhaps Pete's greatest gift to me was that he loved my mum.' David explained that this faithfulness first to David's mum and then to David himself contrasted with his dad's less stable lifestyle. Pete instilled a good work ethic which David sees in himself now. 'He would always help me with job applications and things like that.' He also feels that Mum would have continued to be very protective and would have sought to keep David as her little boy.

David still struggled with identity. Who was he? Should he follow Dad or Pete? For a while he tried Dad's pleasure-seeking lifestyle and looking down on those he felt beneath him. Dad had maintained contact each Christmas, buying expensive gifts, and encouraged David to be like him. But this didn't meet David's need.

Counselling enabled David to 'make sense of the past and gave me the tools to move on. My relationship with Pete is one of friendship rather than parent/child. I am so grateful to him for being there for me and for being my male role model.'

## Time out for children

When emotions are high, and perhaps the child is shouting and arguing, it is often more helpful just to repeat briefly what the required behaviour is and then walk away. Having 'time out' for parent or step-parent and child gives a breathing space for everyone to calm down. In a calmer atmosphere, the issues can be discussed. It is important for every child to be heard. It is for the adults to take the final decisions. Children naturally hit out at those nearest them when hurt and upset. It will help not to take all they say personally.

Young people can be taught, by example as well as with words, that negotiating is the way to solve conflict. They can learn that choosing a suitable time, thinking beforehand about what to say, considering how it might look from the parent's viewpoint, and suggesting realistic solutions will help those in the family and outside it.

## It can work!

Children are children, and many of their behaviours are common to them all. Stepchildren have all these, plus some that come because they have been in a single-parent family and are now in a stepfamily. However, they can all grow up into mature, sensible and sensitive adults, able to form healthy relationships and have positive roles in society.

**To Think About**

Draw a family tree of your children and/or stepchildren.
• How does each child relate to the others?
• What changes has each child experienced?
• How can negative relationships be improved?

CHAPTER 10

# Baby steps

Stepfamily dynamics change again when the couple have a baby of this union. It's a natural urge to have a child with a partner. It joins people together in a special way. However, in a stepfamily there are other issues to consider.

Some couples can't have any more biological children so that makes the decision for them. They may have to come to terms with the feelings of sadness and loss, especially if the step-parent doesn't have children of their own. Wanting to have a child and not being able to is a source of great unhappiness for many.

## A child of our own?

Choosing to have or not to have an 'ours' child is an important subject to discuss. It may need to be considered on a number of occasions as situations and feelings change. One person may have already raised a family and be looking forward to a 'child-free' time, whilst another may have always wanted a large family and this was thwarted by the ending of their previous relationship. Others will decide that they already have enough children. Finances and space in the family home have to be considered too. Choosing the timing of the pregnancy might be possible – though unplanned ones still occur with great regularity! Waiting until the stepfamily has its identity and has settled down is a good idea.

'In terms of having more children, I see the three we already have as my children. I might not be their biological father, but I am a father to them. At the moment we're not planning to have another child. Jenny's getting on with her career. Now we're married she is free to pursue her ambitions, instead of being stuck at home with the kids.'

The thought of having another child to which one is very attached may be threatening to those who have little or no contact with their existing children. Having gone through that heartache, they may be reluctant to have another child in case this relationship ends too.

Perhaps it is for the parent to accede to the one without children of their own? Consider the long-term effects on the relationship if having a child is denied to the partner. But all these are very personal decisions.

## Effects on the children

The existing children in the stepfamily will be affected by the addition of a baby. Often this is a positive experience, linking the family together in a tangible way. But a baby won't necessarily draw the couple or family members together if there are already rifts and divisions. It may even make the situation worse as attention is focused on the new arrival and other children may feel left out. It's natural for siblings to have their noses put out a bit by the new arrival. This jealousy may be stronger for some stepsiblings, especially for the youngest in the stepfamily who loses his position.

This baby is born into a complex family. Everyone will change because of his arrival. The dynamics of the family change. As one father puts it, 'We have a nuclear family within a stepfamily.' Anne Bernstein, author of *Yours, Mine and Ours*, says:

> '**Becoming a mother changed me as a stepmother. It changed how my husband and I shared parental responsibilities for my stepsons... Each had a distinctive relationship with their father and me, and they greeted David [the new baby] each in his own way, accordingly. And I am a different mother to my son than I would have been had I not been a stepmother first.**'

## Teen perspective

Teenagers may greet the news of the pregnancy with horror! They know the facts of life but now they have to acknowledge that their parent and step-parent really do 'do it'. They may feel embarrassed in front of their friends. Others will love the idea of being a little mother or father to the baby. Some will show no reaction, waiting to see how this will affect them before making their feelings known.

> '**My eldest daughter was studying childcare and greeted the news of my pregnancy with, "Good, a real baby to practise on!" The novelty wore off a bit when she had to live with the baby.**'

## Be inclusive!

One of the most important aspects to consider is how to reassure existing children with words and actions that having this child will not mean they are loved less or matter less. This seems to be the worry that half-siblings have expressed the most. Involve all the children in the preparation and care as much as they are willing to be included. Give the reasons why there are any changes to their routine.

'The children even came to the clinic with me and were allowed to listen to the baby's heartbeat. We had lots of discussions over a name and we ended up with two they liked and we liked.'

When David's half-brother was born, he felt things changed and that he was not in the centre of a loving family. 'I knew I was not the first choice, I was not loved in the same way that Jack is. When Pete and Mum moved some years later, there was a room for Jack but not for me.'

'It felt more like a family when Daisy was born. I like going to visit Dad and my stepmum now. There's more to do and talk about. My baby sister's funny, and I get to choose which clothes she wears each day.'

## Different perceptions

The existing children may not understand that caring for babies takes a lot of time and costs a lot of money. They tend to feel that more time and money is being spent on this new arrival, and that they are suffering as a result. Money may be tight, and then when this child is older they may be the only one at home and so more money is available to be spent on them. Older ones may not see this and feel that this young one is being spoilt. Their perception about what is happening may not be reality. Listening to them and explaining the situation will help.

'When I was busy with the baby, my mother-in-law would often take the other three to her home to do some baking. They felt they were special. And my three are actually her step-grandchildren. She's been wonderful with them.'

## The 'ours' child

This 'ours' child will have a different childhood. There may be a large age gap between them and the next half-sibling, so that they grow up within a large family but also like an 'only', without sibling playmates and rivalry. Because this child is born into an older family, they are often very mature and comfortable in the company of adults. Peer friends can sometimes seem rather silly.

Half-siblings are generally very protective of their 'little brother' or 'little sister', though they may also take the role of 'parent' and seek to correct behaviour. The 'ours' child has lots of adults for attention but also to please. Many continue into adulthood to have good relationships with their half-siblings.

'Ours' children may find it difficult to work out how everyone is related. Explaining to friends and teachers can be even harder when not everyone lives in the same house. One family drew a family tree for their 'ours' child to take to school.

> 'Hearing my eldest son, now twenty-two, on his visit to us, call me Dad, our five-year-old "ours" child said, "Does that mean Bruce is my brother?" We hadn't realized that she didn't know just how we are all related.'

> 'But I don't want to be an Auntie. Aunties are old,' said our very upset seven-year-old. She was most indignant that her married half-sibling was going to have a baby.'

Perhaps the most surprising part of being an 'ours' child is that these children can feel different. They do not have a history of bereavement, family breakdown or single-parent family life. These children grow up in the secure existing family structure. However, the other children have had experiences which they don't share. An 'ours' child can feel left out of family reminiscences.

> 'This year we took the two "ours" boys with us when we went with my stepdaughters to visit their mother's grave. It helped them to understand a little that Zoë and Jasmine had had another mummy. The boys thought it must be very horrible to have a mummy die. They soon started playing again, but now they know a little more about their family.'

> 'When everyone talks about when they lived with Mum and her first husband, or when they lived alone, or even when Mum met Dad, I feel left out and alone. I'm the only one who wasn't a part of that.'

## Inclusiveness pays!

As long as the existing children are included as much as possible, and have any changes explained to them, many are happy to embrace the new baby. It is for the parents to choose to treat all the children similarly, even though their love might be different. An 'ours' child can enrich the lives of all the family members.

### To Think About

- How do we both feel about having our own child?
- If age differences are significant, how might older children be encouraged to take a role in the infant's life?

# CHAPTER 11

# Adult steps

When the parent of an adult child forms a new relationship it may not seem like a stepfamily but it is. Adult children who may no longer be living with their parent are still affected by their parent's actions. Parents can be surprised by their offspring's reactions to their new partner. The fact that the children are adult and not so involved in the day-to-day life of their parent doesn't stop them having strong feelings and expressing them in words and actions!

> **Petra was confused by her reaction to the news that her mother was dating again: 'I was most upset – how could she go out with someone else? He might be after her money now she's a wealthy widow. How do I know he's going to treat her right? Has she forgotten my dad already?' It was hard for Petra, and her husband too, as she was moody and frustrated.**

> **Margaret says, 'It all seemed OK till we said we were getting married. Then my son really cross-questioned me. Did I know what I was doing? Was I sure that this was what I wanted? How did I know he wasn't going to let me down? It was like I was the teenager and he was the parent!'**

Anger is often behind such outbursts. People often have angry feelings when they have been hurt. A parent's new relationship may unearth hidden pain from the past. Although they are now grown-up, the feelings of the hurt child can emerge.

Petra's dad died after a long illness. She was very close to him but couldn't grieve as she wanted as she had to return home to another country and care for her own family. She was still mourning her loss and wasn't ready for someone to 'take his place' in her mother's life. Discussing her feelings with a counsellor, she was able to grieve, to find ways to preserve her memories of her father, and tried to see things from her mother's point of view too.

Margaret's son had seen his mother struggle when his father left home. As the eldest he had tried to comfort her and to look after his younger brother. When he got older, Margaret had always turned to him for advice about financial matters and the upkeep of the house. They had made plans for the extension together. Margaret has a new partner and so they are building a stepfamily. Now his feelings are ambiguous. He wants his mum to be happy. He's pleased he won't be so responsible for her but at the same time he's not keen to give up his place in her life. He's genuinely concerned that this new man won't hurt her.

## The challenge of change!

Any change is a challenge. Adult children still see their parents as just that – their parents there for them. When the status quo is upset, they may not be sure how to cope. Home as they knew it has changed. They may be just as unsure how to relate to this step-parent as the step-parent is about relating to these adult children.

'I was in my late teens when Mum married Des. We got on OK but I was ready to move out anyway. I don't think either of us quite knew how we were supposed to relate. It got much easier when I had my own children. Des has his role as Granddad Des, and that works for us.'

Adult children may find it hard to accept a step-parent and may always see them as Mum or Dad's partner. Others will embrace the step-parent and possible stepsiblings and see the enlarged family as fun.

## Inheritance issues

It may seem rather materialistic to refer to inheritance, money and heirlooms but these can cause major rifts in any family and so, also, in stepfamilies. If one family member has lived with the expectation that they will inherit something and this is seen to change with a remarriage, they may feel cheated. Whilst wills are important for all stepfamilies, here it may help to state if a child is still going to inherit an heirloom.

> **'I'm an only child. My father had a number of properties and stocks and shares and I was always told I would be wealthy too when he died. In fact he left everything to my stepmother. She in turn left everything to her friends, so I never saw any of my father's money. I'm angry that she didn't respect my father's wishes.'**

> **'Our children are adult and both our respective partners died. I didn't want to be accused of taking his children's inheritance, so the house we live in is his house and is left to his children. I have my own house which I rent out and this is willed to my son.'**

## Hearing the adult child's concerns

It is the parent's responsibility to make decisions about their life. Answering questions and giving explanations will help. Patience may be needed and the acceptance that an adult child may never fully accept a new step-parent.

'My marriage broke down just before Tom was born. Twenty-five years later I married David and Tom is thrilled. We are a stepfamily. Tom doesn't want to call David "Dad", but they are great friends. They talk the same language, especially as they are both engineers, and have a mutual respect and understanding of each other. It is good for Tom to have a male role model and at times they playfully "gang up against me", which is great to see. Although Tom doesn't live with us he does drop in several times a week. He helps himself to snacks. It is wonderful to see he feels so at home in our home.'

## To Think About

- Consider the emotions your adult child might be experiencing as you form a new partnership.
- What positive thoughts might they have about the new situation which you could build on?
- How might you alleviate some of their concerns?

# Stepping together

# CHAPTER 12

# The 'outside' step

Every stepfamily has another biological parent attached to it. It is tempting to try to ignore this fact and to try to build a nuclear family without this person's influence. This won't work. At least one child in the stepfamily has a link to a biological parent whom they don't live with. The child's relationship to that other parent will affect the stepfamily.

Where the other parent has died, the influence is less direct. However, children may compare their step-parent unfavourably to the dead parent. Photos and memories will mean that this person is not completely absent from the family's thoughts and feelings.

The other parent is frequently seen as the cause for upset in a stepfamily. Some families will have two or more 'other' parents depending on the number of children with different fathers or mothers.

It can be very hard for a step-parent to understand and accept the part this other parent plays in their life. They have no direct link yet their life is affected by the past and present actions of this person. When the contact between the biological parents is good, the step-parent may still struggle with their own reactions to this. They may feel jealous, insecure and left out. Meeting them may also feel peculiar. Tony Parsons, writing in *Man and Boy,* says:

> **'Meeting your partner's ex should be awkward and embarrassing. You know the most intimate details of their life and yet you have never met them. You**

> know they did bad things because of all that you have been told about
> them, and also because if they hadn't done bad things, you would not be
> with your partner.'

Even if there is no contact, this may still affect the child and their relationship with their step-parent. These children may have fantasized about their biological parent, often making them perfect – all they want them to be. This is an unconscious attempt to meet an unmet need to be recognized, accepted and loved by this parent. Although they may have never actually met, the child may still grieve the loss of all the parent 'should' have been to them, and show signs of suffering rejection.

> 'There was the invisible person, like a person off stage, who was my birth
> mother. I was very young when she left us. I think, like most children, I took
> on board that my sister and I weren't good enough reasons for her to stay. I
> wondered where my genes had come from because we had no contact at all.
> At eighteen, I got in touch with my mother. Although initially it was great to
> meet her, I began to realize that she couldn't cope or engage with me when
> things weren't going well for her. She's not a good reference point for me.'

## Working together

It is possible for parents to have a workable relationship with regard to the child and this is good news for all concerned. If both parents and children find the arrangements and relationships are satisfactory then everyone benefits. Then school parents' evenings and so forth can be arranged to suit everyone, and both parents and step-parents can attend the child's celebrations. The child learns that people can disagree but behave in a mature and responsible way.

'For Clare's school play, we sat with her sister in the middle and her mother and stepfather one side, and her father and stepmother the other. Clare was so pleased to have us all together.'

'We go out for a meal to celebrate the children's birthdays now they are older. Their dad comes too, and it's OK. It's a little strange to start with, and what the waitresses make of it I don't know! We can talk about things to do with the children. Because we're in a public place we don't raise any of the problems we might be having with contact arrangements.'

## Warfare

Sadly, when a partnership breaks down, there seems to be an emotional overflow into any contact, and this can have serious repercussions for the child. Contact times can be used as opportunities to air grievances. Arrangements are not honoured and different standards apply in each home, and the child may be subjected to criticism of their parent and step-parent. Pressure can also be brought to bear to encourage the child to want to live with the parent they don't live with most of the time.

Laurie returns from many visits to his mum withdrawn and subdued. It seems that Mum takes the opportunity while Laurie is with her to run his dad and stepmum down. She reminds Laurie that he is not the only child in that family and that he doesn't have to do what his stepmum says. Laurie is told, 'They take my money when they have much more than I have. They're trying to take you away from me. You will become like them.' It takes time for him to readjust to the family he lives with.

Nick desperately wants to have his children living with him. In fact, he took them with him when he left his first wife. The courts ruled that the children should live with their mother. He uses every opportunity to show the children how much better it would be, and all the things they could have and do, if they lived with him. He encourages them to tell him all the things they don't like about living with Mum. Now he has married again he tells the children that if they live with him they would be in a proper family again.

The child might be upset by the relationship they have with their other parent. They may not like the behaviour of their other parent towards them. Check that this is more serious than not liking a ruling (like being in bed by 10 p.m.!). In some extreme cases there may be physical or sexual abuse. This will need intervention by professionals to safeguard the child.

More frequently abuse is verbal or emotional. The child may be deeply affected by, for example, constant name calling. Speaking against those the child loves confuses, unsettles, hurts and angers them. Contact, treats and holidays may be restricted as punishment for their behaviour or that of the other parent. The parent may not have acceptable parenting skills, and act irresponsibly.

## Maintaining contact with the 'other' parent

No one can change another person. So however awful the other parent's behaviour might seem, unless the child is suffering significant harm, the stepfamily will need ways to cope with the relationship with the other parent, and the child will need help and support too. All research points to the benefits of the child maintaining contact with both parents even when this is less than satisfactory.

Children are not divorced from their parents when the parents no longer live together. It may seem easier in the short term to have little or no contact with the other parent, and avoid conflict and upset. However, the child is emotionally attached to the other significant people in their lives, and to break them off from these contacts can generate longer term problems.

Most research suggests that the greatest cause of emotional pain in children following divorce and separation is the ongoing conflict between the parents. If this conflict continues to be frequent, it will disturb the child.

Both interviews with stepfamilies and research with children of divorce show the relationship with the other parent to be a critical one that determines how well children adjust to the loss of one family and to the building of the stepfamily. The attitudes of both former spouses were found to affect the stepfamily in the Cleveland study on reconstituted families by sociologist Lucile Duberman.

It is possible that some children may have contact with former step-parents too, and their behaviour might impinge on this stepfamily too.

There always seem to be rows on the doorstep whenever Stuart calls to collect or deliver the children. However, if Tim takes the children to him or collects them from him, this doesn't happen so much. It seems that the sight of his former wife starts Stuart off on one of his grievances. He hasn't forgiven her for leaving him. So for the sake of peace, Tim drives some distance every other Friday to take the children to their father, and on Sunday drives back to collect them.

Although her stepchildren lived with them, Maxine felt their biological mum was like a black cloud hanging over their family. 'I found out that their mum, Val, was saying things against me to the children. Whenever Val phoned, I felt knotted-up inside. I was really angry with her. Then one day I thought about how Val might be feeling. Here I am having daily contact with her children, hearing all their news, having their friends round for tea, looking after them when they're ill or praising them when they help. If the children keep telling her, "Maxine does this, Maxine cooks us cakes, when we go shopping with Maxine… Maxine lets us…" I think I'd be jealous. Perhaps Val feels she's losing her children and they might reject her for me. Now I feel more sympathy towards her.'

'It might seem easier that we have very little direct contact with my ex. Now the children are older they make their own arrangements to see him. But they do bring their feelings back here. He's had several more wives and girlfriends since he left me. The children now accept that this is how Dad is, but they have been very worried that they might be like him now they have started dating.'

Here are some ways to try to build a workable relationship with 'outside' steps:

- Give the child as much information as possible about the non-contact parent: name, description, personality, what he/she liked. Photos help to make this person real. The child has inherited some genes from this person, so be as positive as possible. Where there has been a death, encourage the child to keep a photo in their room, and perhaps other mementos in a box.
- Accept that contact arrangements may not be fair. The other parent may not do or live as you would wish. The parent the child lives with for most of the time does have the upper hand. Negotiate rather than demand arrangements. Seek to be fair

even when the other person is not being fair. The child will be
watching and learning from you too.

- Have a written agreement between both parents about contact
  arrangements. Discuss these with the child if possible first. Be
  prepared for these to change as the child gets older.

- Give dates of holidays or other events to the other parent in
  writing as far in advance as possible. Always get in touch about
  any changes immediately. This might encourage the other parent
  to do this for you too.

- Consider why the other parent may be behaving like they are.
  Then it might be more possible to find ways to relate to them
  which would help the situation. Don't let your emotional
  reactions dictate your actions.

- Decide as a couple what are your family boundaries – standards,
  behaviour and beliefs. Keep to the decisions you have made as a
  couple about contact with the biological parent.

- Building and maintaining a relationship with a former partner
  may be frustrating and costly but the child will probably
  thank you for it one day. It may take a long time to see any
  results!

- Remember that you have chosen to be in a stepfamily. This
  may mean that you do more than your fair share of bringing
  up the children. The other parent may seem to have all the
  fun while you do all the work. The children are not to blame
  for this.

- Never 'bad mouth' the other parent to the child. However right
  you may be, take care how you explain the situation to the child
  – they are related to that other parent.

- Remember that all this is for the benefit of the child, not the
  parents or step-parents!

'When we first got married, I never thought it would be possible to have a civil conversation with my stepson's other parent. Every contact was a battle. He argued over everything. My wife and I agreed that in front of him we would keep calm and polite. It has taken five years, but recently the three of us were able to sit down together with my stepson to discuss his future schooling.'

'I was angry with my husband's first wife because she had hurt him and her son and daughter. Any contact we had was very strained. I felt she resented me. When it got to eighteenth birthday parties and weddings we managed to be coolly polite. Gradually we have managed to get on better. Now the children have children of their own and we are both treated as grannies. This has made our relationship much easier and we have more things in common to talk about.'

## The 'extended' steps

Grandparents and step-grandparents can be wonderful. Many grandparents will embrace their 'new' grandchildren and treat them as their own. Others will enjoy having the grandchildren they didn't expect to have. Such acceptance will help and encourage everyone. The grandparents' treatment of the new partner and stepchildren will often lead the way for other family members to follow.

'I enjoy my step-grandchildren – they're lovely children. I tell them I acquired them ready grown, although they were only six and nine! I love them too because my daughter does, and I think it's important for her to know her family is accepted just like her sister's own children.'

'We have a great time together when I look after my step-niece and step-nephew. With them with me, I have an excuse to go and see children's films at the cinema! They seem to like having the auntie they don't have biologically.'

Sometimes things are not so straightforward. Some grandparents have been very involved in the care of their grandchildren – perhaps looking after them while the single parent worked. They may have supported their adult child through the trauma of divorce. When this adult child forms a new partnership, the grandparents can feel ousted. They may be afraid their child and grandchildren will be hurt by this new person. They may feel that this partner doesn't live up to their standards or the standards of the previous partner.

Because bonding with biological grandchildren is different to the bonding with step-grandchildren, grandparents may treat them differently. This different approach is particularly difficult for young children to understand. They have acquired these children with a history and were not there at the beginning of their lives. It really helps if the parent and step-parent provide opportunities for step-grandparents to get to know their new step-grandchildren – inviting them for family meals, celebrations, outings or school plays.

Misha became a single parent when her husband left. Her parents were terrific, caring for her son whenever she needed them to. Now Misha is married to Gary, who has two children of his own. Misha's parents have only given their grandson a large sum of money to spend on their stepfamily holiday. Misha and Gary can't afford to give the same amount to the other children. When they all visit Misha's parents, the grandparents treat the children differently. 'I've tried to talk to Mum and Dad but they don't seem to listen to me. They nod but don't change. They keep telling me how to bring up their grandson. I am grateful to them for their help in the past. I've now written to them. If this fails, I will have to explain to the children but this will affect their relationship with these grandparents.'

It is for the grandparents to stand back and let their adult child and grandchild be part of another family. It is for the son or daughter forming the stepfamily to explain to their parents as gently as possible that although they are grateful for all their past support it is now time for change. Explain that it would help everyone if all the children could be treated as similarly as possible, as they are the innocent ones in an adult world.

It may help grandparents and other family members gradually to accept this new partner and children into the family if everyone is included in conversation (for example, when Granny phones and asks how her grandchildren are, the parent includes information about the stepchildren too).

If some of the children are much older, there may not be the same need for them to be treated in the same way.

Maxine's parents were pleased about her marriage but have never treated her stepdaughters in the same way as her daughters. 'As my stepchildren are already in their late teens and have their own grandmother, it hasn't really affected them. It's as though we are sometimes a stepfamily, and sometimes parts of other families too.'

With more people experiencing stepfamily life, there is likely to be more understanding and acceptance of additional family members.

**To Think About**

- In what ways can grandparents be encouraged to engage with the stepchildren?
- In what ways can the stepchildren be encouraged to engage with the extended family?
- In what context could both youngsters and the wider family be able to enjoy each other? For example, days out, attending school plays, holidays, sports (none too arduous for older family members!).

CHAPTER 13

# Step into the future

Everyday living in a healthy stepfamily takes a lot of time, energy, sacrifice and care. It can seem enough just to get through each day. Building in times for fun and opportunities for making stepfamily memories are important too. What is possible and appropriate for each family will depend on resources available and the ages of the children. Doing things together can involve work as well as pleasure. A mix of opportunities with parent and child, step-parent and child, and the whole family will encourage good relationships and give the family memories and stories that will be shared again and again. Children do grow up very quickly, and the chance to do things as a family unit will soon end or at least change to include boyfriends or girlfriends, partners and grandchildren.

Here are some ideas, which each family may consider and then add their own suggestions:

• Find out about the area where the family lives: history, old maps, who lived in the house (using old census information). Pretend to be a tourist in the local area and visit all the sights, museums and other attractions.
• One adult and child cook a special meal for the family.
• Several family members learn a new skill together: playing the guitar, quilting, making greeting cards.
• Go on bike rides together.

- Travel further afield and visit places of interest, go to the beach, explore the countryside.
- Let one family member choose the activities and meals for a day – perhaps to celebrate their birthday.
- Involve the children in day-to-day activities: cleaning the car, mending the fence, sewing on buttons, gardening.
- Decorate the child's bedroom together.
- Arrange family fun days out: bowling, picnics, swimming.
- Care for a family pet together.
- Buy a science kit and do some of the experiments together.
- Climb a mountain together.
- Get involved in a charity together: help with a soup kitchen, help at a children's club, raise money for an organization, fill a shoe box for a needy child.
- Visit the adults' places of work.

'I can see myself now standing at our lounge window. There was my husband and five of our children playing snowballs in the front garden and into the street. Shrieks of laughter rang out. I said to myself, "That's my family – my stepfamily. I'll never forget the scene."'

'Do you remember when Dad started to drive the car down a flight of steps? Do you remember when Neil bought all those inflatable dinghies and tried to sell them round here? Do you remember Mum cooking meat loaf, which you and I hated? Do you remember going to Dad's office in London and being taken out to lunch at that Italian place? I've heard all this when we get together – my children and stepchildren are adult now, but they and we have many memories.'

## Honouring traditions

Mixing traditions can be fun too. The adults and the children may have special ways of celebrating festivals and birthdays and it is good to discuss these in advance of the celebration. Every family has its own rituals and if these are not observed in the stepfamily too it can be very upsetting.

'Our first Christmas together was a disaster! My family tradition had been to get up at a "reasonable" hour, have a huge breakfast together, followed by a time of reflection and prayer, and then open gifts. Gary's tradition was "the earlier the better" to open gifts, and then head off to church. Breakfast? Who wants to eat with so much excitement? In the end my poor stepchildren didn't open their gifts until 1 p.m. or later. To say the least we've compromised and created new "traditions" together, which work for all of us.'

'His children had stockings at the end of their beds on Christmas morning which they could open as soon as they awoke. My two had always had everything downstairs. We added these traditions so they all had stockings – football socks filled with pens, rubbers and sweets, and presents in the lounge which we opened together. Everyone was pleased!'

'We try to be fair, and the children spend every other Christmas Day with us. It's hard on my wife, their mum, as she loves the family traditions of Christmas and can't have her children on a day which is special to her. We have a different Christmas Eve alternate years, when we open family presents together and have a special meal. Then on Christmas Day we go to my parents for dinner so that Moira isn't left with just me all day.'

# What if...?

Sadly, understanding and doing all the 'right' things is no guarantee of success for a stepfamily. Despite the best intentions and the efforts of those involved, some couples aren't able to stay together for a variety of reasons. This can be especially hard on the children, who may have formed good attachments to their step-parent. It is often difficult for step-parents and the extended family to continue to keep in touch. During such a painful time, step-parents can still be significant in the lives of their stepchildren. Relationships that have been built over time do not have to end for ever. It may not be easy to maintain contact but it's certainly worth a try. Children are not responsible for the way adults behave. Even out of difficult situations good can come.

'I had grown very fond of my stepdaughters. We had shared lots of fun together. While Shirley was studying for her degree, I had spent many hours caring for the girls. Then Shirley and I drifted apart. Finally she asked me to leave. I hated leaving the girls behind and they were unhappy too to see me go. They'd already had to leave their father. We've been able to arrange for me to have the girls one Saturday every month which I really look forward to.'

'My husband and I separated and my last memory of seeing my stepdaughter, who by now was eighteen, was over a Chinese meal together. I then went abroad to work for nine years and we lost contact with one another. I often thought of her, had guilty feelings about what had happened and wondered how she, and the rest of her family, was doing.

'On my return to the UK I did the occasional search on the Internet to see if I could trace her, although I was anxious about getting in touch. I felt that I had had little impact in her life and was probably a distant memory.

Then I got an email from her via Friends Reunited. She'd been looking out
for me. As we live in different parts of the country, we've emailed and
spoken on the phone. She is now a married woman and happy and our
conversation was a joyous one, not painful as I imagined it might be.
Rediscovering my (now ex-) stepdaughter was an unexpected moment,
but one I'll treasure.'

Families are never static. Children grow, leave home, go to college,
have their own relationships, marry, have children, and face
difficulties and hurdles. The parents' roles change too. They are no
longer needed as carers and providers as they were when the
children were young. Their roles are more as friends and mentors
and as shoulders to cry on when life is hard. Many will become
grandparents and step-grandparents and the cycle of life goes on.
The everyday pressures of living in and building a stepfamily will
lessen, but that period will affect the relationships that will continue
into old age.

## The conclusion of it all

Every step counts in a building a stepfamily. Those steps may be
large or small, hard or easy, but they are all significant. Sometimes
it seems that one is taking two steps forward and one back, and
progress is slow. Stepfamilies may be formed in practical terms of
living together almost overnight, but to form a cohesive unit will
take years. There are no easy, quick solutions. Every family is
different. But the rewards are great and worth waiting for. Whatever
the past has been for all the family members, the future success will
depend on the quality of relationships within the stepfamily. Then
every step will count.

# Appendix 1

## Meeting the steps

People meet their new partner in so many ways, but often as the friendship develops the question arises of when and how should this person meet the children. Often this can be done quite naturally with other friends and family around so that the meeting is informal and relaxed. Others have to plan this meeting, and parent, possible new partner and children can all be apprehensive! Arrange such a meeting so that everyone has something to do, rather than sitting and looking at each other and making polite conversation. It is for the parent to explain to the children about their friend, giving them time to ask questions and get used to the idea.

There is no perfect time to meet the children, but leaving it until everything is fixed causes the most upset. Some people prefer to wait until their friendship is established so that the children don't keep meeting lots of prospective step-parents. Others will prefer always to let their children know who they are with and where they are going. Whenever and however the children are involved, they tend to see things from their perspective. Be prepared for the children to voice their opinions of the new friend, but encourage them to do this in private!

'It was Christmas morning and my husband and I went to have dinner with my mum. My parents had separated some months earlier that year. When we arrived, we were introduced to Brian. It was clear he was living there. His name had been added to all the present labels. It was such a shock. I hated that day. I would like to have been told about Brian before we visited. It has taken me a long time to accept him.'

'Jenny is the sister of one of my best friends and gradually we got to know each other. From quite early on in our relationship I realized that I had to consider the feelings of the kids. It wasn't just a case of me and Jenny going out. The kids knew me as their uncle's friend before I started going out with Jenny, so they were quite relaxed around me. As I got closer to their mum, I started to develop relationships with them too. One of the most significant moments was when I complimented my eldest stepson on his skateboarding. All I had to say was "Nice Olie" [a move when the skateboarder jumps and takes the board with him, e.g. to mount a kerb]. From that moment he was amazed at how interested I could be in him.'

'Dave would call round as we were going to bed. He would bring my brother and me some sweets. He was very good at reading stories, putting on silly accents and things. We knew how to get him to stay longer talking to us! Then he helped Mum take us with some friends on a birthday outing and he was good fun. We decided it would be OK if he and Mum got together. If we hadn't liked him we would have said.'

'I knew you would marry her the moment I saw her walk up the pathway,' Rob told his dad. Jon had been so worried about introducing Maureen to his teenage son. Jon had invited Maureen in for a cup of tea before they went out for the evening. Rob just about said hello, and then, grunting in his usual fashion, went to his room to watch television. 'He didn't appear to be interested, but he was!' says Jon.

# Appendix 2

## The wedding day

This is a very important and exciting day for the couple. They will be committing themselves to each other in front of witnesses. The children from previous relationships may not view this with the same excitement or enthusiasm. It will be important to plan the event for the couple but with the children in mind.

Further marriages are not so bound by convention as first marriages tend to be. The choices are very wide, and no longer are such weddings 'quiet affairs'. So the bride might be formally dressed in coat and hat, informally dressed, or in a white full-length wedding dress, with veil, carrying a large bouquet. The groom might be in top hat and tails, or in trousers and an open-necked shirt. The ceremony might be in church, a country house or a registry office. It may be in the presence of two witnesses or in front of a hundred guests.

It is for the couple to decide what kind of wedding they want – and can afford. It is usual for the couple to pay for all or most of a wedding when one or both have children from a previous relationship. There are many books, magazines and 'wedding fayres' that will give ideas and possible outlines for the day. If one partner has been married before, they may be content with a simple ceremony. But if one partner hasn't been married before, especially if this is the bride, they may dream of a large traditional white wedding. So discussion about what is wanted and what is realistic is vital.

Neither the cost of the day, nor how grand or simple it is, will determine the happiness or long-term partnership of the couple. The focus of the day should be on lifelong commitment to each other and to the children that one or both partners already have.

If one of the couple is divorced, there may be restrictions on having a wedding service in church. Some churches will offer a blessing to follow the civil ceremony.

The children will need to be considered too. They may have their own views about the day, which might not fit with the 'perfect' vision that the couple or step-parent may have. Involve the children in discussions about the big day, especially about the part the adults want them to have and about what part they want to play. Their suggestions, particularly about dress, may be unconventional but listening to them and considering their views will help them to feel included on the day and will be part of the foundations of your family life together.

A contributor to *Rules of Engagement* by Katharine and Richard Hill stated, 'I said "no kids" at the wedding very firmly to my fiancé. How I wish I had given it more thought. Five years on, my step-kids still hold it against me. I can't think now how I could have been so insensitive and stupid. Please, please warn others.'

The following questions may help the couple work out what is most appropriate for their family on their wedding day:

- Do you want all the children at the wedding?
- Are they able and willing to be at the ceremony?
- Do you want them to be included in the service or ceremony?

- What role would you like each child to have (e.g. bridesmaid, page boy, usher, witness, to 'give the bride away', best man, reading either a Bible passage or a chosen reading)?
- What do you think would be acceptable to the child(ren)?
- Who will be looking after the child(ren) whilst at the wedding?
- Who will have the child(ren) to stay so that you may have a few nights alone?

The children can be included in the prayers, in additional vows, by giving a gift, lighting a family candle or a circle of candles – one for each member of the family.

'We had quite a traditional wedding. My daughter was a bridesmaid, and my partner's son was a page boy. We both promised in the service to love and care for each child. As my former husband had died, we did invite his parents too. It was a bitter-sweet day for them. They were happy for us.'

'We "eloped" abroad and married with just two witnesses. The children really felt left out, and we have since had a ceremony renewing our vows with our children and family present.'

'It was a perfect day, and everything went smoothly. We had lots of family and friends. But in hindsight, I wished I had prepared the children more.'

'My eldest daughter would only come to the wedding if she was allowed to wear jeans! I reluctantly said yes, and she came which was the most important thing. She even smiled for the photographs!'

Because at least one of you has children you might also consider:

- If widowed, would it be appropriate to invite your former in-laws?
- Are you going to invite other children too? (Some couples arrange for a children's entertainer during the reception to amuse the children.)
- When and how would it be best to tell your ex-wife/husband about your wedding? You may need their co-operation regarding the children. You should pay for all the children's outfits and accessories for your wedding even if you pay maintenance to their other parent.
- Consider where everyone will sit, both at the ceremony and at the reception if having a 'top table'. You may change any tradition, but do let guests know in advance if it might affect them.

'In ancient Persia newlyweds are said to have drunk honeyed water to ensure a frisky future. Hence the word honeymoon' (quoted in an article in the *Telegraph Magazine* on 14 August 2005). Having a honeymoon takes on a new slant when there are children around!

The practical issues of finance and childcare may dictate what is possible. Many couples have a short break without the children and then take everyone on a family holiday later. Others include the children in a 'family-moon', where everyone goes away together to celebrate. For those who choose to marry abroad this is particularly popular.

The romantic picture of an idyllic stay in an exotic location may have to wait till the children have grown up!

'After the wedding, we realized that all the photographs of us had at least one of our children in too! We did get away for two nights on our own, as friends looked after the children. It was the first time I had left my four-year-old since she was born. It did give us just a few precious hours together before we coped with family life.'

'We planned our wedding in just five weeks – it was very different from our first weddings, informal and inexpensive but much more fun. The emphasis was on us and our children.'

# Further Resources

## References

Bernstein, Anne C., *Yours, Mine and Ours*, W. W. Norton & Company, 1990.

Chapman, Gary, *The Five Love Languages: How to Express Heartfelt Commitment to Your Mate*, Northfield Publishing, 1995.

Einstein, Elizabeth, *Stepfamily*, Random House Inc, 1985.

Hill, Katherine and Richard, *Rules of Engagement*, Lion Hudson plc, 2005.

Kübler-Ross, Elisabeth, *On Death and Dying*, London, Tavistock/Routledge, 1992.

Lawton, Jan – Research psychologist, Stepfamily Project at the University of Queensland, a major government study of behavioural interventions for stepfamilies with troubled children.

Nance-Nash, Sheryl, 'Managing a Blended Family', *Black Enterprise*, Volume 34, Issue 7, Feb 2004. p. 87ff. Article on the Questia Media America Inc. site: www.questia.com.

Parsons, Rob, *The Money Secret*, Hodder & Stoughton, 2005.

Parsons, Rob, *21st Century Marriage* – DVD and workbook (new for 2007).

Parsons, Rob, *21st Century Parent* – DVD and workbook (new for 2007).

Parsons, Tony, *Man and Boy*, HarperCollins Publishers, 2000.

Tufnell, Christine and Worth, Jill, *All Alone – Help and Hope for Single Parents*, Spring Harvest, Paternoster Publishing, 2002.

## Resources from Care for the Family

*Connect2* – this unique five-session course can be run in your local community or church to support and encourage couples in the early stages of their marriage.

*From this Step Forward* – marriage preparation course for life in a stepfamily by Care for the Family.

*Life in a Stepfamily* – Care for the Family's network supporting Stepfamilies, including a free newsletter three times a year, resources and informal opportunities to meet with others.

*The Money Secret Workbook* – a companion to *The Money Secret,* written to help you take the concepts presented in the book one step further.

## Counselling Agencies

Association of Christian Counsellors
29 Momus Boulevard
Coventry
CV2 5NA
084 5124 9569

British Association for Counselling and Psychotherapy
BACP House
St John's Business Park
Lutterworth
LE17 4HB
0870 443 5252

Relate
0845 456 1310
www.relate.org.uk

## Useful websites

www.childrensgrief.net (Linda Goldman)

www.chimaeraconsulting.com/tuckman.htm

## Speakers at Smart Marriage Conference, Dallas, Texas, 2005

Dr. Francesca Adler-Baeder (author of *Smart Steps*).

Ron Deal of Successful Stepfamilies and David Olsen of Prepare/Enrich: Results given at Smart Marriages Conference 2005, not yet published.

Gordon Taylor (co-author of *Designing Dynamic Stepfamilies*).

# Care for the Family

Care for the Family has been supporting and encouraging families in the UK since 1988.

Its family-building events have been attended by over 275,000 people and many more have been helped through special initiatives – including stepfamilies, bereaved parents and those parenting alone.

Founded by best-selling author and speaker Rob Parsons, the charity is committed to strengthening family life and helping those who face family difficulties.

If you would like to hear more about our national family life events, encouragement for your family and receive help to make a difference in your community, please write to us today.

 Care for the Family, Garth House, Leon Avenue, Cardiff CF15 7RG
(029) 2081 0800
or visit us online at www.careforthefamily.org.uk

All Lion books are available from your local bookshop, or can be ordered via our website or from Marston Book Services. For a free catalogue, showing the complete list of titles available, please contact:

Customer Services
Marston Book Services
PO Box 269
Abingdon
Oxon
OX14 4YN

Tel: 01235 465500
Fax: 01235 465555

Our website can be found at:
www.lionhudson.com